FIRE
YOURSELF

WILLY STEWART

Fire Yourself by Willy Stewart

BDI Publishers

ISBN: 978-0-9962646-7-9

Second Edition

This is a work of fiction. Any resemblance of characters or persons living or dead is purely coincidental.

Cover Design: Tudor Maier
Layout Design: Tudor Maier

BDI Publishers
Atlanta, Georgia

dedication

TO SHERRI,

my wife, partner and best friend.

table of contents

introduction

Introduction by G. Brent Darnell, best selling author of The People Profit Connection

The Fire Yourself movement is about a new generation of business leaders rising up to demonstrate their strength and leadership through services and love. When you fire yourself as your own higher power, you abandon your egotistical, controlling, self-centered leadership and submit your life and business to God's authority, vowing to serve others.

When I first met Edward McLand, the CEO of McLand Construction, quite frankly, I didn't like him. I finally realized why. It's because I recognized the things in Edward that I didn't like about myself. But the story begins there. By the end of this leadershift fable, Edward McLand is transformed from an egotistical, controlling, self-centered person to a warm, generous, caring person who is ready at a moment's notice to serve others.

When you fire yourself, you will discover the same thing that Edward did, that it's possible to have success and peace, love and strength, productivity and balance, all at the same time. It's not only a great story, but there are very practical surveys and methodologies outlined in the book that will help any business to thrive.

chapter one

FIRED UP

It was Friday afternoon and Manhattan was bustling with the kind of traffic noise, chatter and activity that created the explosive symphony of sights and sounds unique to New York City. Still, the noise of the city paled in comparison to the firestorm of thought in the mind of 45 year-old construction business leader Edward McLand, CEO of McLand Construction.

As he exited the posh high-rise building close to Union Square Park where he'd just concluded a heated round of contract negotiations with a developer, Edward's thoughts were rampant and his frustrations were high. The deal would contract his company to build a mixed-use development project in the northern suburb of Savannah, GA, where McLand Construction was headquartered.

As he replayed the day's discussions in his head, with each passing moment, Edward grew more frustrated that he was not better able to manipulate the outcome of negotiations. Known for his aggressive business acumen, losing was never an option. Edward was upset and mentally drained as he attempted to hail a cab to take him to the airport.

He wore the frustrations of his day like the well-tailored suit he donned on his five-feet, 11-inch, lean frame. Edward impatiently waved a hand at passing taxis to no avail. Amazingly as it may seem, in a city dotted with yellow vehicles everywhere, finding an empty taxi was a project in itself. Then, as if he still had the thick long hair of his youth, he slid that same hand across the side of his head near his lightly sprinkled salt and pepper hairline. His olive skin tone worked well with the gray that was starting to fill in. Work had taken the place of his youthful obsession with his good looks and attractiveness to the opposite sex, but Edward still carried a little of that conceitedness with him.

Just as he began to mumble about how much he hated this city, a yellow cab slowly pulled over to the curb where he stood. Edward had barely eased in the backseat before he was on the phone with Joe Palmer, his Director of Business Development, yelling and cussing about how those Yankees thought they could take advantage of a southern construction company.

McLand Construction was a mid-sized, $100 million-a-year construction company founded and operated by Edward himself. The company primarily built commercial buildings, including offices, retail and mixed-use projects. And like many companies, McLand had been hit hard during the economic downturn. His company had shrunk to about half of what it had been just a few years earlier and had been barely able to stay afloat. Slowly his business, and professional esteem along with it, seemed to be slipping through his fingers. Having lived his life with a need to prove his worth and desire to belong, the downturn had impacted his ego as well as his relationships. And his lack of control over any of it made him angry with himself and everyone around him.

Edward was so preoccupied with his own thoughts that he wasn't fully aware of his surroundings. He did pause long enough, however, to notice the cab driver's accent. With disdain, he quietly murmured questions to himself like, why the hell are cab drivers in New York City all foreigners and rude?

With not even a nod of acknowledgement, Edward abrasively instructed the driver to take him to JFK airport. He continued his rant on the phone with Joe, blurting a recap of the meeting and how the developer had asked him to lower his price by three percent. This basically amounted to the profits they had anticipated making on the project. He resented that he couldn't afford not to accept the miserly offer, as he needed to keep his employees busy, not to mention he needed to pay down the debt he had accrued over the past few years. Joe, at the other end of the phone knew well enough to take it all in quietly, as he had done many times in the past and more frequently in the last couple of years. Joe had become Edward's emotional punching bag.

As they entered the Queens-Midtown tunnel to cross the Hudson River, Edward lost cell phone reception. So not to lose the momentum of his tirade with Joe, he tossed the now useless phone on the seat next to him and continued to vent to the driver, who quietly listened.

Unlike most passengers who take solace in the momentary calm of the dim, soundproof tunnel, Edward was uneasy and anxious. Halfway through the tunnel, they noticed red and blue lights ahead as the traffic came to a halt; there had been an accident in the tunnel and all lanes had come to a stop to allow for the accident vehicles to be removed. The thought of missing his flight and having to sit in a quiet tunnel trapped with his own thoughts and feelings made Edward feel claustrophobic and that infuriated him even more. With few options left, he engaged the driver in a one-sided conversation.

Edward noticed from the laminated piece of paper hanging on the back of the passenger seat that the driver's full name was Pablo Cervantes. Pablo appeared to be in his early sixties.

Edward questioned Pablo in a terse voice about how long he thought the ride would take as if Pablo had the power to estimate or control an accident delay.

Edward couldn't miss his flight because he had an important business meeting back home, and he expected Pablo, traffic and the universe to accommodate him.

Pablo, with a Spanish accent and the most soothing voice Edward had ever heard, responded with a reassuring smile that they should be moving shortly.

Edward was somewhat surprised by the calming effect Pablo's voice had on him. His interest piqued enough to ask Pablo where he was from and how long he had been in the U.S.

Before Pablo could respond, Edward unexpectedly felt the unction to share with Pablo his dilemma with the business and the contract. Edward was a notoriously poor listener and had a very low emotional intelligence when it came to self-regulating his impulses and interruptions.

Once traffic started moving and he regained cellular reception, Edward once again called Joe. This time they discussed a potential project they were chasing that required a special use permit, which would also mandate engaging the influence and support of one of the local politicians.

When Joe mentioned that the politician might not be able to help, Edward once again went on a tirade. He reminded Joe that the politician was obligated, since he had given a huge amount of money to the politician's campaign had supported him through tough times and even held a fund raiser for him; that was not acceptable, and he would have to handle this one personally. The conversation continued with Edward demanding better performance from Joe and everyone on the management team, it was time to perform or get off the bus.

Through the conversations he overheard, Pablo observed Edward's selfish and egotistical leadership style. He could tell Edward wasn't the kind of man who would readily take advice from anyone, least of all a taxi cab driver. Because of this, Pablo didn't share his background as a highly successful business owner in his native country. Edward probably wouldn't believe him anyway. Most people Pablo met in the U.S. didn't. He knew firsthand what it felt like to watch a business unravel before your eyes and have an entire staff depending on you for their livelihood. An unfortunate turn of events had led him to the United States, and he'd never been able to regain the social prestige or wealth of his former life. Pablo had grown to accept and even embrace his new, simpler life, but he still found it tough to resist sharing with Edward, and others, all that he had learned through his experiences.

With the final threat of "getting off the bus", Edward hit the "End" button on his phone abruptly and with the same show of disgust he had displayed earlier, he threw the phone on the seat next to him just as Pablo pulled in front of the double doors leading to departures.

"How many kids does he have?" Pablo said as Edward snatched the phone back off the seat to prepare himself for the mad dash through the airport and security, which he, like everyone else in this world, detested.

"Huh?" Edward replied confused, slightly irritated and already in hustle mode to make his flight.

"Joe. It sounds like he's your right-hand man. How many kids does he have?" Pablo asked in his soothing tone and with an easy smile.

Edward was totally perplexed, but was in too much of a hurry to entertain this any longer. "Two, I think. No, maybe three and a stepchild, so I guess that would be four, huh? It's strange to say, but I guess I don't know for sure," he finally admitted as he shoved some bills through the divider window.

As Edward threw one leg out of the taxi, Pablo turned around and asked Edward if he could share one piece of parting advice.

Edward nodded impatiently as Pablo said in a serious, urgent tone, "In order to find real significance in this world, you need to do just one thing. All you have to do is fire yourself as your own Higher Power."

Edward was confused by the words but astonishingly touched at the same time. He was in deep thought as he stepped out and closed the door behind him. His intent was to lean back through the window to question Pablo, despite the risk of missing his flight. However, by the time he set his carry-on on the curb and turned to face the taxi, he saw the Allied Cab sign merging amongst all the other yellow taxis leaving the drop-off area. And just as quickly, Edward disappeared amid the army of gray and black suits, each heading toward his own important destination.

"Life", he said to himself, "would be so much easier if I didn't have to board another plane in my life."

chapter two
FIRE!

As Edward sat on the plane, he remembered the words from Pablo: "Fire yourself as your own Higher Power." As a businessman, the idea of ever firing yourself just sounded ridiculous, but the second half of the statement made him ponder. Had he been acting as his own Higher Power? What did that even mean? Was he acting as his own god or that he was in such control of his life that he did not need a god? He leaned his head back and thought, I go to church, well sometimes, I volunteer when I have the time, I love my wife and kids and spend time with them, again, when I have the time. I would not consider I am my own god, ridiculous.

He chuckled as he shook the thought out of his head and pulled out documents to prepare for his meeting in Savannah. Before he could concentrate on the papers in his hand, Edward's aisle mate was squeezing by him to claim the window seat. The young lady apologized for the disruption and quickly took her seat, just in time for takeoff.

Edward introduced himself and quickly went back to work. Out of his peripheral view, he could see she was just as focused on the Cosmopolitan magazine she was reading while she was plugged into her music. What a waste of time, he thought as he went back to his problems and the anticipation of changing planes in Atlanta – the busiest airport in the world. There was no telling which concourse he would arrive at and how far he would have to run to catch his next flight to Savannah, it was always an anxious mystery.

In the week that followed, Edward received an emergency call that an office building his company was building and was partially complete caught on fire and a volunteer fireman died while helping to put the fire out. Initial reports were claiming that the sprinkler system, which had been already tested, did not operate as intended and an investigation was being opened to determine if the construction company and the manufacturer were responsible for the defective performance. Edward went through the roof at the news, demanding to know who were the project manager and superintendent on the project and threatening to launch his own internal investigation in addition to the many that had already been launched. The State Fire Marshal, OSHA, and plaintiff attorneys all had multiple certified fire investigators on site. Even the State Bureau of Investigation was looking into the situation to determine if arson played a part in this terrible disaster.

A quick internal and preliminary investigation uncovered that the owner and contractor changed the specification in the design drawings and selected a less expensive system with fewer sprinklers and controls. It was unclear whether this was a violation of the building permit and whether it led the system to fail.

Edward and his assistant spent the day on the phone with his corporate attorney setting up meetings and arranging for experts to come and assist in the investigation. In addition to attorneys, a meeting was immediately set with a public relations firm to develop an internal and external communication strategy. Tomorrow was going to be an intense, anxious and stressful day, one that Edward was not looking forward to. In the midst of the New York developer challenge, this was the last thing he wanted to deal with, a public relations crisis.

As Edward sat in his office alone that evening, he did what he had found himself doing often since his New York trip. Even with all the background noise of his current situation, he remembered the voice of Pablo saying, "Fire yourself ..." With the recollection of these two simple words, he decided to find out the name of the fireman who died in the fire. He felt a sudden urge to pay a visit to the victim's family. He headed for the bar down the street to soothe his pain and stress the only way he knew, red Italian wine.

"What do you mean I cannot go and visit her and pay my condolences", yelled Edward. He was meeting with Alexander Bradley and George

Miraldi, his attorneys, and they had strictly forbidden him from reaching out to anyone associated with the fire that was not working for them. They had also found out that the widow had hired a personal injury, ambulance chasing, attorney who was making a lot of threats and noise. They told him he had to wait until the investigation was over regardless of his compelling need to go see the widow. Period.

After asking Michelle, his assistant, to do some digging, she informed him that the young man's name was Bill Danford and that he'd left behind a wife and three young kids. Without saying a word to anyone, especially his attorneys, Edward drove to the widow's neighborhood. He had to find out for himself where she lived, and perhaps if it was meant to be, he may just see her out in the yard.

The humble neighborhood was very different than the sprawling mini-mansion that he and his wife Victoria owned. This was a neighborhood of one-story, brick, ranch houses similar to those that were built all over the US and were extremely popular with the booming post-war middle class of the mid-Twentieth Century. He found the house and after driving around the block a couple of times he pulled in the driveway. To his surprise, Mrs. Danford was home and answered his knock holding a one-year- old baby, with a three-year-old tugging at her dress. A five-year-old boy was hiding in the shadows.

Edward hesitated and changed his mind about telling her who he was and instead identified himself as an attorney looking to represent her on the wrongful death claim of her husband, and she let him in. He wore a hat and sunglasses.

As he looked around and noticed the worn furniture and rugs, peeling wallpaper and faded paint, a deep sense of sorrow washed over Edward. He looked above the fireplace mantle and saw a collage of family photos in chipped and cracked frames and a gorgeous wooden cross with the word "Hope" written below it. He was at a loss for words. The meeting didn't last long as she explained to him that someone had already come by and she had signed some papers committing to a contingency representation. Basically, she didn't have to pay him any money if he didn't win or settle the case, which was a good thing for she had none. Edward said little and left her humble home, tears streaming down his face. Right before he left, she actually said that she was concerned for the owners and the others involved in the project and that she had been praying for them.

Driving back to the office, he was totally perplexed at how someone who had just lost her spouse could project so much love, humility and forgiveness. He had never seen or experienced anything quite like it. This woman, in her humbleness showed a deep sense of inner strength that Edward could only wish for. He wondered what did she have; what did she believe in; how could those sad eyes communicate so much care and gentleness, and so much love?

When he returned to the office, it was business as usual. Everything was the same outwardly, yet inwardly things were beginning to feel slightly different to Edward.

With the ongoing investigation, a potential lawsuit, trying to win work and being squeezed by the New York developer from any potential profits, Edward felt like the walls were closing in on him. To make matters worse, his relationships with his wife and kids were strained and reaching breaking point. Just the previous week, Edward had been totally consumed with work and had missed his eleven-year-old son Eddie's soccer game where he'd scored the winning goal. He was in the office in a Saturday meeting with his management team strategizing the future of the company and completely forgot about the game, even though he had promised both his son and wife that he would meet them there. That happened the same week he missed Hannah's piano recital while he was in New York. It seemed he just didn't have any margin in his life to enjoy what really mattered.

His wife's comment to him after he apologized profusely while at the same time justifying his absence was, "Edward, you are a smart guy who has a lot of head knowledge but no love in your heart. Life is full of choices and you are making the wrong ones."

He felt deflated, as the words permeated the atmosphere and his heart. He was a bit surprised at his own reaction to his wife's harsh words. Typically, as long as there were no immediate repercussions, he figured his loved ones should just understand that he's a busy guy with a ton of responsibility. But this time was different. He needed to find a way to change her perception.

For the first time in his adult life, he cared what someone else thought, and also for the first time, he clearly saw his own self-centeredness. Sadly, he agreed with his wife and knew he needed to figure out a way to shift his way of dealing with others from his head to his heart. As Edward watched his wife getting ready to take the kids to school, he was left pondering, once again just how disconnected he was from the people he loved the most.

"We are out of cream, so if you have a minute from your very busy schedule, pick up some at the grocery store", she said sarcastically as she stormed out and slammed the door. Standing there alone in that big, beautifully decorated room, just reminded Edward of how much he hated to be alone with his own thoughts and illuminated just how lonely he really was. What he would have given at that moment to be back in the dingy, two-bedroom flat feeling the peace and love of the widowed Mrs. Danford.

He decided to find some peace with a walk through Forsyth Park or River Street in downtown Savannah. He decided on River Street; he never grew tired of studying the trees with hanging Spanish moss that adorned nearly every street along his commute through the historic district.

After nearly 30 years of residence in the quaint, cultural cove known and loved by many tourists, Edward still felt comforted and captivated by its beauty and charm. The cobblestone streets and unique architecture of the riverfront area gave him a plethora of scenic distractions from all he was contemplating.

As he strolled along in his own thoughts, somewhat feeling like he was losing grip on everything that mattered, he noticed Mrs. Danford leaving the laundromat with a bag full of clothes with three kids in tow. His first thought was that he couldn't imagine not having a washer and dryer at home and having to haul all the clothes to get them washed and dried at an old, dated and dirty place. The little things we have taken for granted and no longer compute in our minds. He hesitated, as his attorney's demands not to speak with her still resonated in his mind, but then gave in to what he clearly believed was the right thing to do; he walked towards her.

"Mrs. Danford, let me help you with the bag."

"Oh, you are the attorney that came by my house, I never did get your name. Thank you, you are very kind. I didn't realize just how difficult life would be with Bill gone." With tears welling in her eyes, she said, "I miss him so much!"

Edward, again hesitated but launched into it not knowing what was going to happen. With a slight stutter, he said, "Mrs. Danford, I, I am not really an attorney. My name is Edward McLand and I own the construction company that was building the apartment complex that caught fire where your husband, valiantly died fighting the flames. I am so sorry for your loss and I am sorry I lied to you. I am under strict orders by my attorney not to talk to anyone associated with the accident until the investigation reveals what happened. I am truly sorry ma'am." Tears flowed like an open faucet. He'd never felt this way in his entire life.

She reached and grabbed his hand and burying her face in his chest she started to sob. The two kids pulling at her dress were asking what was wrong and the one on her arms started to wail.

Edward, worried what people around would think with the ongoing scene, started to pull back. Mrs. Danford somewhat composed herself and with swollen yet caring eyes looked at him and said, "Mr. McLand, you seem to be a good man. Bill knew the dangers of the job; I am certain the good Lord has a purpose for all this. It is really hard to accept and understand now, but we must not lean on our own understanding and trust Him with all of our heart."

Edward could not believe what he was hearing. Why wasn't she punching and cursing him? Why isn't she yelling at him and blaming him for what happened? What did this woman have that he just could not comprehend?

They walked in silence to her car and after putting the laundry bag in the trunk, he started walking away and then turned towards her, "Ma'am, I promise that I will make it right for you and the kids. Whether we are at fault or not." He started to walk away and found himself looking at the beautiful blue sky, dumbfounded with what just happened.

He spotted a gas station across the road with one of those awful so-called convenience stores, and he remembered "get cream" so he crossed the street and entered once again into his world.

Back at the office, Edward closed himself in his office and refused to talk to anyone. He sat at his desk unable to concentrate, thoughts of Mrs. Danford and her kids swirled in his mind like a hurricane; "What is happening to my life?" he asked out loud. Then Pablo's final words, right before he got out of the cab, came rushing in: "fire yourself to have significance in this world". What was that all about?

There was a knock on the door and Edward yelled, "Leave me alone!"

"It's Joe. Edward, this is important, we have to talk right away."

Joe opened the door and walked into Edward's office and noticed that it was a mess, papers, files all over his desk and on the floor. This was bad, Joe thought to himself knowing how anal Edward was about keeping everything in order, there would never be two unrelated pieces of paper touching each other on his desk.

"I just got off the phone with John Paul and he is cancelling the project. He heard about the fire and is concerned with the bad PR something like that will bring. He said he is not going to take that risk; the project is already a risky proposition!"

"What? I can't believe it! And I thought things couldn't get any worse. Tell Michelle right away to get me on the first plane tomorrow morning to New York. I cannot let this happen. And tell that Yankee asshole that I am coming to see him and with all the work we already have done on this project he better be there to see me. Or I will tear his office door down!"

Edward was steaming. His sadness turned to fury, but deeper down, it was pure fear. Fear of failure, fear of losing it all, and fear of staining his name and reputation. He sat back down, staring at the ceiling not knowing what to do; his mind was in a fog, too many bad thoughts racing through his head. Then Pablo's face appeared; "I have to talk to him, yes, I absolutely need to talk to him," he said out loud to himself.

Edward remembered the name of the taxi company and after doing a Google search, he called and asked the operator to send a guy named Pablo with a Spanish last name to pick him up at the airport.

Edward got home late after meeting with his staff to go over all the details of the project he was going to New York to save. Victoria was sitting in the living room with the lights out as he walked by heading to the fridge for a much needed beer. "Another long and fun day at work?" she asked sarcastically.

"I thought you were asleep", he said as he turned on the light and noticed the glass of wine and the empty bottle beside it.

"No, I also had a long and fun day. This is for you." She tossed a manila envelope towards him.

"What is it?"

"We are done, I am done, the kids are done. Done with you. Those are divorced papers. Very detailed divorce papers," she said in a very terse tone as she started walking up the stairs.

"Wait a minute, you just can't spring something like that and walk away. You have no idea what I am going through. If you did, you wouldn't be doing this. Come on Vickie, let's talk – this is crazy!"

"Don't Vickie me. You're a sorry excuse for a husband. And father. You don't have a clue what is going on with your family; you've never cared enough to know," she yelled from the top of the stairs as pillows and blankets came falling down.

Edward took a swig of the beer and slammed it against the wall across the room. Just when he thought things couldn't get worse, they did. He sank into the couch and passed out from total exhaustion.

chapter three

COMMITMENT TO SERVE

Pablo arrived at La Guardia to pick Edward up and told him that was is an incredible coincidence that he could even be there to collect him. He explained that it was a scheduled day off from work but two drivers had called in sick causing him to be called into work. Edward, frankly, was in no mood for a lengthy conversation; his mind was focused on the upcoming meeting and what he needed to do and say to save the project. Traffic crawled as it usually did on the way to the city. Edward's curiosity finally got the best of him and as they drove to midtown Manhattan, he asked Pablo what he meant by the statement, "Fire myself as my own Higher Power."

Proceeding with no caution or hesitation, Pablo explained to him what he had witnessed during the one hour they were together. And he did so with the kind of wisdom that caught Edward off guard but also made him stand up and pay attention. Pablo explained that he observed the behavior of a selfish leader who lacked compassion and love for people. He had the characteristics of someone who had to win at all costs and thought people were mere pawns in his own game to be used and discarded as needed.

Pablo added that true success in this life is measured by how many people we love and what kind of legacy we leave behind. This kind of deep commitment to serving others comes from the soul and is only possible when we are in a committed relationship with God. Pablo recounted that Jesus tells us to "Love the Lord your God with all your heart and with all your soul and with all your mind. This is the first and greatest commandment." And "Love your neighbor as yourself."

"So you see the instructions are simple. Not easy, but simple," Pablo said.

Not liking where the conversation was going, Edward quickly retorted, "Pablo, come on, this may work in church, and frankly I am not sure if it even does there. But what does firing myself as my own Higher Power have to do with love?"

"You see Edward, it has everything to do with love. Because in order to love others, you must first love yourself, and to do that, you have to be true to yourself and recognize that this love comes from the heart and soul and not from the brain. This deep self-actualization can be elusive because our own ego gets in the way. Not until we surrender our life to serving others and stop being our own higher power can we then be lifted up. Paul talks about love in the Bible when he says, "Love is patient, love is kind. It does not envy, it does not boast, it is not proud. It does not dishonor others, it is not self-seeking, it is not easily angered, it keeps no record of wrongs. Love does not delight in evil but rejoices with the truth. It always protects, always trusts, always hopes, and always perseveres. Love never fails.

But where there are prophecies, they will cease; where there are tongues, they will be stilled; where there is knowledge, it will pass away. And now these three remain: faith, hope and love. But the greatest of these is love."

"So Edward, when you fire yourself and shift your leadership from an egotistical leader to a servant leader, then you will find true success."

"Edward, it starts with loving those you work with. The love I am talking about here is one where because you love them, you make an intentional and significant effort to elevate them so that they can reach their goals, dreams and aspirations in business and in life. At the same time, with that same love, you have to make tough decisions and let go the ones who do not embrace a culture of empathy, compassion and forgiveness."

"Pablo, I hear what you are saying, but I am running a complicated business in a very complicated and competitive industry. This stuff just wouldn't work. Love is great, but it is not going to win me work; it is not going to help me meet payroll; it is not going to put food on the table, and it is certainly not going to put my kids through college."

"I agree, Edward. There is a lot more to running a business than love, but it is the foundation on which to build. You also must have a clear purpose and direction of where you are going and how you are going to get there, as well as an unwavering discipline in execution to bring it all together. But it starts with love, which leads to a level of trust among your people that is seldom seen in companies today."

Totally forgetting he was talking to a cab driver and not noticing an accent now at all, Edward was confused. He was confused about what was being said to him and equally confused about his own internal response to the words. None of this made sense, yet at the same time, it made perfect sense out of the chaos of his world.

"Pablo, you talk about love and Jesus and all that stuff, but why is there so much chaos and hate in this world? Seriously, why isn't God doing something about it? If he is so powerful and can change the world, why does he allow all this suffering to exist, all these wars and destruction, all this death?"

"Because sin is man-made and because this suffering is created by man. Why should He clean it up?"

Edward thought for a moment, "Because he is God!"

"How much time do you have? Do you have time for an illustration?" asked Pablo.

"I do, my meeting is not for another hour, why?"

Pablo got off the highway and pulled into a gas station convenience store. "Hey Nick, how are you this morning?"

"Really Pablo, again?" replied Nick with a bit of sarcasm in his voice.

"Edward, what cereal do you like? Cheerios, Frosted Flakes, Special K?"

"Come on Pablo what is this all about? OK, Cheerios."

Pablo grabbed a box of Cheerios from the shelf, opened the box and bag and poured the cereal on the floor, spilling it all over the aisle making a huge mess.

"What the hell, Pablo, what are you doing?"

Pablo handed Edward a broom and dust pan, "here, clean it up."

"You have got to be freaking kidding me, right? No way!"

"Why not?" replied Pablo.

"Because I didn't make this ridiculous mess, you did!"

Edward caught himself, dumbfounded. "OK, I got it. Now who the hell is going to clean this up?"

"Hey Nick, here is a twenty, sorry about the mess."

As Nick grabbed the twenty from the shelf, he looked at Edward and said, "He does this all the time."

"Sir, we are at your building. Would you like me to pick you up this afternoon and take you to your hotel?" Pablo said in his signature soothing tone and resurfaced heavy accent.

Edward was still lost in thoughts of the previous statement, forcing Pablo to repeat himself. Finally, Edward nodded his agreement and told Pablo he would call him once the meeting was over. Having to be reminded to pay his fare, Edward absent-mindedly swiped his card in the device hanging in front of him before grabbing his briefcase and sports coat.

Stepping out of the taxi, neither the crisp early morning air nor the commotion of New York pedestrians shook Edward out of his contemplative daze. He was able, though, to remain focued throughout the morning, especially during the meeting where he was able to convince the developers to keep him on board as the contractor, after all, there was an investigation going on and it wasn't clear exactly what happened. He told them that it would only take two-three weeks for the preliminary results of the investigation to be announced and if McLand was at fault, he would remove himself from the project. It took all the charm, charisma and groveling Edward could muster before they agreed to put the project on hold until the findings were known.

Edward left the building and decided on a short walk to clear his mind and compose himself inwardly. They may not have noticed, but Edward was worried sick and suffering from an internal anxiety that he was able to mask, just as he had done with his deeper feelings all his life. He blended into the crowd of what is truly the heartbeat of the world. The hustle bustle of New York cannot be explained in words, he thought, you have to experience it in person. As he strolled down Fifth Avenue while at the same time trying not to get run over by the busyness and urgency that everyone displayed, he decided to reward himself with a New York hot dog. Why not, he thought, for whatever reason they tasted fantastic in New York.

As he continued to think back to his conversation with Pablo, he realized the words fire yourself had moved him. He also started to wonder who this

character Pablo really was and how did he know
so much? Edward made a mental note to ask him
when he saw him later that afternoon.

chapter four

STROLL IN THE PARK

At the end of his walk, he called Pablo, and he came and picked him up. Not quite ready to go to the hotel, Edward asked for suggestions on where he could unwind from his day. Pablo suggested a stroll in Central Park. It was spring and the late afternoon weather was the perfect combination of sunshine and breeze. Central Park was just what he needed to mentally debrief the details of his many meetings and strategize his next business maneuver.

Edward instinctively reached for his cell phone ready to unload his opinions of the day's discussions on his trusted advisor, Joe Palmer. Instead, the sound of Pablo's voice and the gaze of his watchful eyes were interrupting him.

"Calling Joe? Did you ever find out how many kids he has?" Pablo said with a knowing smile.

"Pablo, my man, if only you knew the literal and figurative fires that awaited me when I got back to Savannah, you wouldn't ask such a random question. Let's just say he has the same number of kids he had the last time you asked," said Edward in a slightly condescending and dismissive tone, secretly hating that he hadn't remembered to ask when he returned home and embarrassed that he had been caught by Pablo appearing insensitive again.

Once again, Edward found himself caring what someone else thought of him, and this time, it was a complete stranger, a foreign cab driver at that. He questioned whether he was going mad and thought back to his earlier talk with Pablo. With this thought and the need to escape the disapproving stare of Pablo following his last comment, Edward decided to invite Pablo to take a walk with him through the park. He was curious to hear what other words of wisdom this peculiar man might be able to impart.

"Edward, it is nearly impossible to find a parking space in the city, and even harder close to Central Park. I do know someone that works as a bellman a few of blocks away; he will let us park in the underground parking garage for a couple of hours."

As they walked, Edward began his questions. "Pablo, what is this love of which you speak? You talked about a different kind of love. I understand the words, but I can't quite grasp the concept. The love I know is expressed with money or in a physical way."

"I know what you mean," replied Pablo. "The world has taken a truly powerful word with so much meaning and watered it down. Let me tell you how love matters in your business."

"First of all, it starts with you," Pablo continued. "It starts at the top and you have to build a team of people that embrace these same ideals and principles. Being a loving leader, a servant leader, doesn't mean you are a weak leader; in fact, it is the opposite. Meekness is not weakness, it is power under control. It is having enough confidence in who you are that allows you to be humble, loving and empathetic. So building a great company requires building great relationships with your people, making a positive impact on their lives and those who they touch. That is why I asked how many kids Joe has. Your inability to answer this question shows how shallow the relationships are with even those you depend on the most and them on you."

At this point, Edward nodded in agreement and asked Pablo where he was from and where his knowledge on the subject came from.

Pablo replied, "I was born in South America many years ago. I have been around the world and have experienced much. It is a long story and if it's okay, we can leave that story until the end. There is much we need to accomplish."

They found a bench with the perfect view to sit back and admire the beauty of the park in the spring, with trees coming back to life that framed the incredible New York skyline and white flowers blooming everywhere. Edward was amazed that this calm oasis could sit in the heart of a chaotic, fast-paced and energetic city. He observed the diversity of the visitors and the commonality of respect for the peace and beauty of this place. Whether black, brown, white, young, old, educated or homeless, no one appeared out of place here.

The two college students debating philosophy between kisses were just as "at home" in Central Park as the group of six-year-old, field trip students. From the businessman too preoccupied with his iPhone to notice the teenager next to him crying as she read a letter from someone, to the bike riders and skateboarders, everyone seemed to be content in their own piece of this world. Pablo seemed to be the only one even aware of the others around him.

Pablo broke the silence. "You see Edward, you need to surround yourself with people who love and are passionate about what they do and who love working with you and your company."

"I hear what you are saying. But passion is so overused in this world, and frankly, I am not sure anyone really knows what it means. We all have to get up in the morning and go to work because we all need a job. It's how we survive at the most elemental level – food, clothing and shelter. And I would say that most of the people I work with do not dread going to work, but being passionate about it is a different story."

"Well, Edward, are you passionate about what you do in your business? Are you going to work on the balls of your feet? Are your people going to work on the balls of their feet?"

He pondered for a moment, going back in time. At one time he loved what he did. Unfortunately, it was for the wrong reasons. Work became like a drug. It was his escape from a family life that he could never connect with, a family he felt no relational tie to. It wasn't that he did not want to, but he was afraid he did not have the capacity to love. After all, he was never nourished growing up; basically, he was an adult by the age of 12. The oldest of three brothers, much of the household duties fell on him. His father was a salesman and was on the road Monday through Friday and was always exhausted on the weekends. Spending time with his sons was not a priority. He would on occasion attempt to be with them, but not often enough for Edward to feel loved or protected. He was never nourished with love as a child. There was not a memory bank of happy scenes and loving moments; no scenes of family vacations, no scenes of gatherings with laughter and joy. Even holidays like Christmas or Easter were a mere blur, like they never happened, and to this day, celebrating them with the warmth and love that others showed was just not in Edward's being. Sad, very sad. He resented his father most of his adult life, blaming him for his inability to connect with his kids and with his wife. Blaming him for the insensitive heart he developed, nothing more than a shield of protection to mask insecurities and feelings of abandonment as a child. Now he was perpetuating a cycle created by his own upbringing. By the birth of the third child, his mother felt abandoned, lonely, and overwhelmed. This led to long bouts of depression for her, where just making it through a day became an agonizing experience.

Even though Edward had sworn to himself that he would never be like his dad, in a different sort of way, he had fallen into the same cycle. Even though he did not travel the way his dad did, being involved with his business and several philanthropic boards kept him away from home almost every night. It was always justifiable in his mind. He needed to wine and dine clients and potential clients, or he needed to be known and seen as a leader in the community so he could win work. To make matters worse, he had a standing leadership meeting every Saturday morning, something he justified as the only time of the week when they could meet and not be disturbed. Everyone on his team hated this meeting and resented the fact that their weekends were being highjacked.

Remembering Pablo's question, Edward responded, "I am not certain if I can say that I am passionate about what I do for the right reasons. I get a tremendous amount of satisfaction with work; it fills my ego and uplifts my self-esteem if things are going great. But I'm just starting to realize as we talk about it that this so-called passion is coming at the expense of others, including my family."

"Edward, it is clear that your life is out of balance. In fact, the lives of most senior leaders in organizations are out of balance. Unfortunately, their lives are defined by their work and their success at work. I am not implying by any means that work is not important. It is the consuming effect it can have on your life and the life of others around you that can prove toxic."

Just then, a flock of birds gathered on the stone right beside the bench on which the two men were sitting. They were all different sizes, but they all looked alike, except one. This one had brilliant colors, especially compared to its black and brown shaded flock mates. It was beautiful. Just as both men's attention was drawn to the distinct look of the one bird, it swooped down and picked a worm from the grass. With a meal in tow, it quickly flew off, with the rest following. They were gone. Edward commented that he'd never seen a bird find its meal before. Pablo smiled as he had seen this often and always took it as a reminder that his daily needs would always be met.

Pablo continued. "So once again, living a balanced life goes back to having the right people performing at their best, at their unique ability so that you can then do the same. Basically, focus on what you are best at, and let others do the stuff that takes away precious time that could be spent with your family and yourself."

As they sat on a bench, Edward was leaning back looking up at the sky, taking in every word and pondering for the first time in his life all the time over the years he had spent at work away from those he loved. He could not remember the last time he spoke with his two brothers or his parents. The intention was always there. Making time for it just had not been a priority. He was known for forgetting birthdays and always had the right excuse for why he couldn't attend a family gathering. He barely made it to many of his own immediate family activities. And when he did, it was not uncommon to find him outside of the house or away from the crowd of family or friends on work-related calls.

Pablo sat and watched Edward wrestle with his thoughts, and he knew right then that his words were beginning to penetrate.

He continued, "You see, Edward, balance is not necessarily the chore of keeping an equal number of hours on the three legs of the balance stool – work, family and self. It is working smart; it is building relational esteem with your spouse and kids, and it is learning to spend time with yourself, which for most CEOs is the most difficult one. When it comes to oneself, it is an art to consciously balance and embrace the four pillars: the mind, the body, the soul and the community. It is important that you make time to feed the mind with good literature, to stay abreast of the latest news and technology and to engage in spirited and exciting conversations. This may mean even taking the time to play mind- exercising games such as crosswords or number puzzles. Exercising the mind has been proven to keep you thinking clearly into your senior years. You should make it a habit of reading ten pages of a good business, leadership or personal development book every day, there are many worth reading. And it is just as important to be physically active."

Edward recalled for a moment when he used to love to run. It was part of his baseline in life and one of the activities that lowered his stress. He knew that he could always resolve any issue he was dealing with after a long run through the woods. That was many years ago. He couldn't remember the last time he had gone on a run, and his waistline was clearly starting to show it.

He thought of all the statistics he'd read about the state of Americans' health regarding obesity, and he felt that if he didn't do something about it, he would join those ranks soon. But where he would find the time was the question.

"Even more important than exercising the mind and the body," continued Pablo, "is to find quiet time every day to spend in prayer connecting with the Lord. The soul needs spiritual food, manna that will sustain your ability to embrace the fruit of the Spirit which is love, joy, peace, forbearance, kindness, goodness, faithfulness, gentleness and self-control. This is the foundation of a servant leader, of a loving husband and of a dedicated father."

Edward quickly thought about how he'd grade himself as a servant leader, loving husband and dedicated father. The results were so dismal that he had to immediately shake the thought out of his head and divert his attention in a different direction.

Edward turned to Pablo pensively and asked, "You said there were four. There's the mind, body, and soul, but what's the other one?" He fixated on his monogrammed cufflinks and shiny Italian shoes. They both felt displaced outside on this bench in Central Park.

"Oh yes, community. This is the one often overlooked, but we'll talk more on this later. As far as your company, in addition to having passionate people working with you, let me share with you two more essential needs in building a loving, high-performing team within your organization. There is also the need for clarity and trust. By clarity, I simply mean each team member is clear about his role, his responsibility and accountability in his job and to the team. They also have a clear understanding of the company's mission, vision, and short and long-term goals. And once this clarity is gained, the individuals come together to work cohesively toward those common goals.

"On a personal level," Pablo continued, "you also need clarity in your life. It is imperative that you identify your purpose, basically the "why" in your life. In other words, really knowing why you exist and what you are meant to do and accomplish while you are in this world. Edward, I can assure you that at your eulogy, and I can assure that there will be one, you will not be recognized by your business accomplishments or how hard you worked or what a great problem solver you were. Here is the question that matters, will they be proclaiming what a loving, caring and compassionate person you were?"

Pablo let that last statement sink in.

chapter five

CLARITY

Edward understood. Although Pablo was speaking primarily about business strategies, the last statement staggered him and immediately Victoria and his kids came to mind. Business was the world he understood best, but right this minute it all seem irrelevant, Edward's thoughts were on the events at home and he realized just how much he needed his wife, Victoria, even when she continually exposed his weaknesses which he resented and did little to improve.

He thought of the many times she'd dragged him to marriage counseling complaining about his inattentiveness to the family, lack of real intimacy, emotional unavailability, this or that. She had said more than once, "I don't know what we're doing here. I feel like we're living separate lives. I feel very alone in this marriage. You are not even a good roommate." She often made these declarations with tears in her eyes while Edward watched confused by the emotionalism and wondering what in the heck she was talking about.

Didn't she understand that everything he did was for her and the family? He worked as hard as he did to provide a good life for his family, but his intentions never seemed to be clear to her. He didn't understand her complaints. He wasn't perfect, but he was a hard-working man who loved his family, but he couldn't achieve his business goals, retire early enough to enjoy his grandkids, and be at every family function at the same time. This lack of clarity on both sides kept them frustrated and disgruntled. Two ships passing in the night.

Likewise, the aggressive growth goals he had set for McLand Construction were not purely selfish ambition. He often stayed up at night pondering the best ways to keep the income of his employees stable and how to improve the long and short-term benefits the company offered. Expansion meant more opportunities to promote and employ. As CEO, there was no need to share this. He could relay his mission and vision in one word. Growth. Wasn't growth the goal of every company? His reasons or method shouldn't have to be explained as long as payroll was being met, or so he had thought all this time.

He suddenly saw how his assumption that his plan and intentions should be obvious to those around him had permeated in his home and business life, causing confusion in both. He had almost forgotten Pablo was there when his thought was interrupted.

"Starting with a clear mission and vision statement is the first step to clarity and is not as easy as you might think. Once that's developed between you and your leadership team, it needs to be clearly communicated to your team and gained their understanding and agreement. Then you can proceed with a growth strategy. But implementation of each goal will also require buy-in from your team each step of the way.

"The mission statement should answer the question: this is what we do, for who and how. It should be simple where you do not need to memorize, it is what McLand is all about. The vision statement is an aspirational statement, basically, where do you want to be say, ten years from now. And frankly, it doesn't have to be just about growth and revenue. Edward, success is defined as 'the progressive realization of a worthy ideal.' So you and your team need to decide what that ideal is and articulate clearly.

"Edward, you also need to understand your purpose in life. Basically, identify the 'why' of your existence. The why, your purpose, lies at the convergence of your mission and your vision. While your mission, as I explained before, answers what, who and how, and your vision answers the when, your purpose answers the why."

"Pablo, please stop. Why, what, who, when, ideal, mission and whatever else you said is too much to remember right now. I need to write this down."

He reached in his coat pocket and pull out an empty note card with the company logo on it and started to scribble.

chapter six

TRUST

Pablo continued, "Clarity is just the beginning. A team is truly formed when cohesiveness comes into play."

Edward stiffened his relaxed body posture and raised his index finger in protest. "Pablo, I have a very cohesive team. I run a tight ship, and everyone in leadership is aware of what the other teams are doing. We work together well and before the economic downturn, we had the bottom line success to prove it."

Detecting Edward's defensiveness, Pablo softened his tone and exhaled slowly. "Cohesiveness in one word translates to trust. A cohesive team is one where there is an enormous amount of trust between the members. Cohesive teams not only work together for the overall success of the group, but they genuinely trust each other as they do it. Do you implicitly trust each member of your team and they you?"

Edward responded thoughtfully. "I trust them not to breach confidentiality or do anything to discredit me or the company. Is that what you mean?"

"Yes, in part, but members of a cohesive team truly like each other and protect each other's backs," Pablo responded. "They are willing to be vulnerable, knowing that they won't be shot down. This team engages in serious debate and disagreements in arriving at the best solution for the issue at hand. Do you trust them with your ideas and vision for McLand?"

Before waiting on a response, Pablo continued "They debate passionately along ideological differences leaving their egos at the door. Once a decision is made, team members quickly align their thinking and actions with the decision and support it wholeheartedly, and then they move on to the next issue."

Pablo softened his tone even more as he turned to face Edward. "This team makes decisions quickly and with the foundation of love and the fruit of the spirit, everyone is encouraged and expected to participate. The leader of this team facilitates the conversation but does not control it. It is truly a group effort. Members of the team come prepared to the meeting and are disciplined about doing their homework and preparing ahead of time."

Edward was confused and was still bordering on defensiveness. "What does trust, love and 'spirit fruit' – whatever that is – have to do with discipline and preparation for one of my meetings? The two have absolutely nothing to do with one another, and for Christ's sake, what does love have to do with the way I run my business? None of this makes sense!"

Pablo was patient in his explanation. "With trust as the glue that holds the members together, no one feels as though they have been ignored or overlooked during discussions. No one goes to the water cooler and vents if their idea or suggestion was not well received. There is a sense of maturity and a great deal of respect for one another, which breeds discipline and one hundred percent effort and participation. This incredibly successful team only happens in companies where the trust and respect comes from the top and filters throughout, and where leaders understand the concept of servant leaders who care for everyone in the organization.

"Absence of this kind of trust is a portal for jealousy, egotism, discord, blame, cynicism and sarcasm. Members are afraid to disagree or be vulnerable with their thoughts and ideas. Everyone is guarded, and passive aggressiveness becomes prevalent and vying for position and power becomes the norm. This is what you don't want, my friend," Pablo said as he stood up. "One more thing which, frankly, is even more important; do you have this trust I just described with Victoria?"

"Pablo, sit down for one minute. No, I don't and it is leading to a divorce. I just have a hard time letting her in; I just feel, what's the word I am looking for, inadequate – that's it. There is a feeling that I have to prove myself in everything that I do, even at home. I am afraid of being vulnerable, of feeling insecure. You know, exposing my weaknesses. Which has become very clear today that there are plenty."

"Does she trust you Edward?"

"She does; it drives me crazy sometimes. She is an open book, and there is no doubt that you know how she is feeling and where she is coming from each and every time!"

"You have a good one Edward, don't let her slip away. Believe me, that is a gift and seldom happens in marriages, which is the reason that over half do not make it. Trust is the foundation of a solid and long-lasting marriage. If you love her, save it my friend."

And with that last statement, Pablo got up and started walking away.

"Pablo," Edward yelled, "I'll walk to my hotel from here, pick me up in the morning."

Pablo, without turning back, just waved and kept going knowing that he needed Edward to soak the conversation on his own. Which Edward did for the next hour.

As he was leaving the park, he noticed the FAO Schwartz store on the corner next to the Apple store.

Never one to bring gifts for his children from a business trip, Edward thought that a toy for his son could serve as a small token to make up for some of the missed soccer games. He was sure there would even be something there for his fourteen-year-old daughter, Hannah. He'd missed his share of her art exhibits as well, even the big one when one of her pieces was featured at the Savannah College of Art and Design. With several, huge, busy floors, this was a toy store on steroids. Edward even found himself reconnecting with his inner little boy. As he passed the floor piano, he remembered the movie Big with Tom Hanks and the scene where he and his co-star jumped on it and did an awesome routine to the delight of the shoppers and moviegoers. He contemplated stepping on it for a second but brushed off the thought as foolish and childish. As he walked away, a father and son duo stepped on and started to play it totally off key while laughing so hard that the whole floor could hear them. Edward looked back as he walked away and thought to himself that he needed to bring Eddie – he would love that. Of course, they would have to see the movie first.

While picking up a few toys for his own kids, Edward thought of the fireman's widow and threw a few extra things in the cart for her little ones.

The next morning, Pablo was waiting outside the hotel as instructed, but the ride to the airport was a quiet one. Edward's mind had raced in the hotel all night long thinking about Victoria wanting a divorce and the effect that would have on the kids and his reputation in the community. He also contemplated what would happen to McLand Construction if the investigation proved them guilty; he was certain that they could not survive the blow. The recession had left them financially weak, and they were just starting to recover, there were no reserves or back-up plans at this time.

And then, Pablo and their stroll in the park. He once again wondered who this man Pablo was and where he came from. He and Pablo didn't talk much during the ride to the airport. They were both deep in thought about all that had been exchanged in the park the day before. As he swiped his credit card in the payment device hanging in front of him, Pablo finally broke the silence.

"It's again been a pleasure, my friend. As soon as you fire yourself as your own Higher Power, all that I've said will make more sense and you'll see the positive changes happen."

There were those words again, simultaneously haunting and comforting Edward.

chapter seven

YOU'RE FIRED

Edward boarded the plane in hopes of a quiet, disruption-free flight. He needed to be alone with his thoughts, something he was becoming increasingly comfortable with.

Subconsciously, Edward did a five-second assessment of the likelihood of peace and quiet by sizing up his nearby travel partners. There was a lady speaking Spanish behind him with a child. Then there was the tall, robust gentleman across the isle loudly making small talk with anyone within earshot, and an athletic, energetic-looking young man wrapping up a phone call seated near the window to his left. This would definitely be a flight for earplugs. He moved into his seat with a nod toward the young man, who introduced himself as Caleb.

As the plane started its descent towards Hartsfield-Jackson Atlanta International Airport, Edward immediately noticed the slight change of pressure in his sinuses. This was something he had been dealing with for some time, and other than the dreaded surgery, nothing had been able to help. A moment later, he watched the copilot come out of the cabin with what appeared to be a flashlight in his hand as he made his way toward where Edward was sitting. As he passed his row, he stopped and kneeled down, peeling back the carpet exposing what looked like a porthole hatch. After a couple of attempts, the copilot finally opened the porthole, which exposed a roaring sound from the underbelly of the plane. Edward made careful observation, as all this was happening near him. The copilot shined the flashlight through the porthole for a couple of minutes before closing the hatch and replacing the carpet. He then headed back to the cabin. At this point, most everyone who noticed was perplexed and expecting an announcement from the captain.

A few minutes passed, and once again the copilot came walking down the aisle to the same spot and repeated his previous routine, looking intently into the inside of the fuselage. Again, he left the scene without a word. At this time, you could hear a pin drop from the eerie silence inside the plane. Three or so minutes passed, which felt like an eternity, when the captain's voice came over the intercom. "Ladies and gentlemen, we have a grave situation. We have been able to visually confirm that the landing gear is down; however, our computer is telling us that it is not locked in place. There is no way to confirm whether it is or isn't. We have radioed the control tower and have requested an emergency landing. Before we can do that, we will be circling for about 45 minutes burning the excess fuel we currently have. Our very capable flight attendants will describe in a few minutes what you will need to do regarding the emergency landing instructions."

The lady sitting in the row directly behind Edward started to panic speaking in Spanish and asking what was going on. She didn't understand what the pilot had just announced – she assumed it was serious by the dead calm that engulfed the plane.

The young missionary sitting beside Edward turned around and started explaining to her in broken Spanish what the captain had said. She started to cry, and in between sobs, she shared with the young man that she was taking her granddaughter back home with her to Puerto Rico for a short visit after being in New York for a few days for her son's wedding.

The young man, who Edward was guessing was about 25 years old, told her that he was on his way to a one-year mission trip to Peru. He was leaving his job as an up-and-coming trader on Wall Street to pursue a life of significance in this world.

Seeing that the little girl was getting scared, Caleb turned around and reached over the seat and held the child's hands and prayed softly in Spanish. Even though Edward could not understand what he was saying, he felt it deep within his soul; he then felt a tear running down his cheek. He could not remember the last time he had cried. He wasn't sure if he ever had.

His thoughts were interrupted by the flight attendant's voice explaining that in twenty minutes, she would show everyone the emergency landing posture and exit instructions, with an assurance that this was just FAA authorized precautions. There was a commotion inside the plane as people came to realize the gravity of the situation. Sobs and sounds of panic could be heard throughout the cabin.

Edward's mind raced in many directions. First and foremost, he thought about his wife and two kids and what life would be like for them without him around. Had he left them enough life insurance? What would happen to his business? Could it sustain itself without him? It had crossed his mind from time to time, but he had no perpetuation plan in place. Death was not something he'd planned for or thought about in any detail until then.

As he sat still for a few seconds, which felt like long minutes, he heard Pablo's voice in his head. "Fire yourself as your own Higher Power."

He felt the warmth of the dead fireman's widow when she held his hands in prayer, as he witnessed Caleb's sense of peace and assurance of his place beyond this world.

Edward, who had never prayed before, bowed his head and whispered, "Lord, it is evident from the actions of the last few weeks in my life that you exist. How can people in the midst of chaos and pain feel this kind of peace through you; how can the widow forgive me with so much love, how can this young man be experiencing a sense of inner peace when death could be calling? Lord, I ask that you forgive me for all the wrong that I have done; Lord, I ask that you forgive me for all the people I have hurt and all the pain that I have caused; Lord, I ask that you forgive me for thinking that I could do it on my own, for living a life searching for power and finding nothing but empty feelings and an unhappiness that only I knew. Lord, right now, I am firing myself as my own Higher Power. I am laying my life at the foot of your cross and if, God, it is your will that we survive this landing, I will seek You and honor You for the rest of my life!"

When Edward lifted his head up, he noticed the young man looking at him with a sweet smile and knowing nod of approval. Even though there was a feeling of dread in the air, Edward felt a sense of calmness that he didn't remember ever experiencing. He felt what he thought must be peace.

His thoughts were interrupted by the flight attendant explaining that when she gave the word, everyone must lean forward and put their arms around the back of their legs tightly. Once the plane landed, everyone should proceed to the nearest emergency exit and, in a calm and orderly manner, approach the door and slide down the rubber shoot by placing both arms on their chest and jumping feet first, the attendants would be there to help as well as those sitting in the emergency aisles who would be given additional instructions.

The wheels of the plane touched the runway like a feather. The pilot had lowered the plane's speed to the minimum possible and approached the landing as horizontal to the runway as possible. Edward felt the landing even less than he would under normal circumstances. The plane coasted across the entire length of the runway with the pilot just touching the reverse thrusters to slow it down. When the passengers realized that the plane was coming to a full stop, everyone started yelling, clapping and crying.

Edward smiled and turned to the young man and gave him a hug. Caleb looked at Edward and said with an authority beyond his years, "The Lord has a plan for you. Let it happen; don't fight it."

With the emergency lights of ambulances and fire trucks flashing through the windows, the pilot explained that it would not be necessary to do an emergency evacuation. The maintenance crew was inspecting the landing gear and preparing to tow the plane to the gate. Once again, claps erupted with a prevailing sense of relief. Death had come close, but it obviously wasn't anyone's time to go that day.

For Edward, the near death experience had served another purpose. He considered himself officially fired.

The second leg of his trip to Savannah was uneventful. He thought about Victoria the entire trip and what he needed to do to make things right with her. He just could not lose her; he was in love with her even when he had a hard time demonstrating it. Living without her just could not possibly happen. Just before landing, he looked in his brief case and there it was, the manila envelope with the divorce documents. He didn't have the strength to open it and put it back and softly said to himself, "Lord, I need some help here, I don't know how to fix this mess I have made."

Instead of going to the office, he went straight home but no one was there. He then remembered that Eddie's team was having a make-up soccer game after school and he headed to the game. He parked, and as he walked towards the field, he saw Victoria with Hannah in the stands with a couple dozen parents, all intently watching the game.

Without saying anything, he walked onto the sidelines and spoke with the two coaches, who then called the referee and the game was stopped. Everyone in the stands and all the players were dumbfounded as to what was going on. Then Edward started yelling, "Ladies and gentlemen, I'd like to take this opportunity to apologize for the interruption. The game will resume very shortly I promise. My name is Edward McLand. I'm married to one of the most beautiful women on earth. In my hand, I hold the divorce papers she gave me a couple of days ago." As Victoria and Hannah covered their faces with embarrassment, Edward continued, "Now this isn't her fault, it is my fault. All of it. I have not been there for her and the kids. We are married, but I have been a stranger." As people stood and started taking pictures with their phones, Victoria put her arm around Hannah, still not knowing what to think of the incredible scene she was witnessing.

Edward continued, "I am here to ask my wife Victoria, my daughter Hannah and my son Eddie for their forgiveness. Something incredible has happened to me that has changed my life forever, and I want to share it with them."

Pointing at Victoria, Edward said "I want you to experience what I've experienced. Vickie, I love you, and I'm asking for one more chance. Let me clean up my mess. Let me show you that we can work things out; that I can work this out."

Victoria stood up and with a cracking voice responded, "Edward, I can't. I've given you other chances before and you have broken every promise you've made!"

"Keep the papers, I have signed them. If I break this promise, you can file them. Come on, I am begging, what do you say? All these people are my witnesses! I am not going to hurt you or the kids again."

Victoria yelled back, "No more Saturday morning business meetings, no more missed soccer games or recitals. You will be present in our relationship – we come first!"

"No, you and the kids come second!"

The crowd groaned and you could hear a pin drop.

"No, it is not what you think. I fired myself, God comes first from now on and you all come second! "

Victoria was still standing hesitating what to do when Hannah stood up and said, "Come on Mom, what do you have to lose?"

With the crowd watching and the coaches and referee looking at their watch and impatient kids starting to move around, Victoria ran onto the field and embraced Edward and gave him a passionate kiss. Hannah came running behind her and Eddie was already next to his dad. They embraced in a family hug and tears fell everywhere. The crowd started clapping, yelling and whistling and the game resumed.

Victoria, holding Edward's hand, asked, "How did you get them to stop the game?"

"McLand Construction is sponsoring both teams next year - new shirts and soccer balls!"

They both laughed as they made their way to the stands

chapter eight

LEADERSHIFT HAPPENS

Edward returned to his daily routine, but there was an undeniable centeredness there that had eluded him before. He hadn't taken his moment of firing himself on the plane lightly, but he also wasn't sure how changing himself and changing his way of leading his company was supposed to look. So Edward went about his busy days, waiting on the answer and trusting that it would come naturally.

It was Friday afternoon a week after the landing from his last New York trip. Edward was about to pass his assistant's desk leaving a meeting when he remembered something related to his standard Saturday meeting. "Michelle, please send a memo to the leadership team reminding them to bring ideas for the new brand promise we are working on to tomorrow's meeting."

As she responded affirmatively already typing the memo, Edward could overhear Joe Palmer explaining his dilemma to his own assistant.

"Is there a time slot next Friday I may be able to break away and go with her? It's bad enough I can't make it to most of Ellen's Friday chemo treatments, but she's usually so sick on Saturday, it kills me to have to leave her for these leadership meetings. Thank God for my mother-in-law or I wouldn't have anyone to watch the four boys. Oh well, I guess me getting myself fired would just worsen the situation, huh?" Joe said with a forced chuckle, reciprocated by his assistant whose sympathetic eyes told a different story.

Hearing the words, "Getting myself fired" and hearing his colleague's personal dilemma for the first time were both jarring to Edward. They had

had countless working meals together, meetings and business trips, and they had even played golf with other staffers once or twice. How could he not have known that Joe's wife had cancer and was undergoing chemotherapy? Four boys? He just knew there was a girl in there somewhere, and the foreign sound of Joe's wife's name also made him feel ashamed.

Pablo's question about how many kids Joe had came back to Edward, and suddenly he understood how out of touch he had been as a leader, and even as a husband and father.

When Edward returned to himself, he realized he was still standing at Michelle's desk, and she was about to hit the send button on the memo. He startled her by saying with an urgent tone, "Stop! Please change the memo to cancel Saturday meetings indefinitely, effective today. Whatever was on the agenda, please find time Monday for us to meet."

By then, Joe had left his assistant's cubicle.

Edward walked over to Jade's desk as if involuntarily and unconscious of what his own body was doing. "Jade, I couldn't help but overhear your conversation with Joe a minute ago."

She was about to interrupt to question how he was able to hear, considering the distance between the areas, but thought better of it and let him continue.

"I had no idea about Ellen. Michelle is sending a memo that the Saturday meetings are cancelled. I'd like you to also clear Joe's schedule on Fridays for the next month. Send a list of his appointments and duties to Michelle, and she and I will disperse coverage between me and the team." With that, he walked off still somewhat dazed.

Per his instruction, Michelle was busy the rest of the day arranging for flowers to be sent on behalf of the company, placing an FAO Schwartz order for Joe's boys and coordinating a babysitting service to help the mother-in-law on Saturdays.

Edward went home and hugged his own wife, Victoria, a little tighter, and as he looked in her eyes and gave a heartfelt apology, he knew his termination had begun. He was beginning to see himself and the people around him differently, and it was a good feeling. After the apology and embrace, he asked his wife about her day and really listened.

She reluctantly began to share some details but opened up a little more when she noticed he was really paying attention. Victoria graduated in the top 10% in her class at the University of Georgia with a degree in math. She taught 8th grade math and technology at the public school that Eddie attended. She was not one to bring her work home; Edward never seemed interested in hearing about her day and what the kids were learning. She was passionate about education and had helped propel the school to one of the top schools in the city and in the state. With enthusiasm, she shared with Edward the new software the kids were learning and how amazed she was that kids in the eighth grade could pick up this stuff so quickly.

He then relayed the story of Joe and Ellen, and to his surprise, his wife not only already knew, but she had gone to sit with Ellen on some of those Fridays that Joe was caught at work.

As Victoria saw the surprised look on her husband's face, she gently stroked the back of his hand and said, "Edward, he's been the backbone of your company for more than a decade. How could you not know?"

He slowly shook his head, suddenly seeing in himself what Pablo had seen during that first taxi ride.

The rest of Edward's week went smoother than usual. He was feeling a little lighter on the inside going into a new week as he continued to practice the act of firing himself daily.

The Saturday meeting had been moved to Monday, and he was looking forward to testing some of Pablo's theories on implementing clarity and cohesiveness in his leadership style. The strategic and collaborative nature of the Monday morning meeting made it a great place to start.

Edward had always kept the challenges the company faced, as well as the future goals and objectives, under wraps for the most part, even from his top executives. But he vowed to himself to try a different approach.

He opened the meeting with an inspirational quote and motivational words about making the week a great one, rather than his typical strictly business demeanor. He perceived some of the surprised looks and smirks in the room and for a moment regretted not sticking with what he was most comfortable doing. He continued in the clarity and cohesiveness vein by sharing the news of the low profit margin of the mixed-use development project recently negotiated in New York. The deal was not yet inked as the developers were waiting on the results of the fire investigation, so he opened the floor for ideas regarding his conundrum of the little or no return on investment for the project.

To his surprise, Philip, his VP of Finance, was a masterful but unassuming negotiator who offered several brilliant ideas about how to position the deal to the New York developers. Philip had worked in Boston for a large developer and had been involved in a number of complex deals. As most accountants, Philip was an introvert who loved playing with spreadsheets and structuring the numbers part of the deals. He seldom spoke at the meetings, but when he did everyone was always surprised as to his insights and clear understanding of the problems being discussed.

Edward immediately decided to take Philip with him on the next trip to help close the deal, and he couldn't believe he had not been aware of these hidden talents.

During the rest of the ideation session, he also realized how valuable a five thousand foot view could be in assessing business problems and coming up with viable solutions. He had been so deep in the weeds that he had not been able to step back and look at the entire company and the value each of his members brought to the meetings. These were really smart people and he had not been challenging their brains and expertise. He thought that that was going to change going forward.

He had surrounded himself with experts that were smarter than him, and yet he had not allowed them to flourish.

The meeting was concluded with a brainstorming session on a new business pitch going forward.

They concluded that they needed a brand promise that they all would learn and be able to articulate. It was clear to all that the company needed to freshen up the brand and modernize their look as as well as create visual continuity across all their outlets. Someone suggested a social media campaign since they currently did not have a Facebook page or a Twitter account. It was decided that Joe was going to reach out and set up a meeting in the next couple of months with a branding and marketing company. Everyone felt energized with the new openness and strategic nature of the meeting. Unlike their typical weekly meeting that focused primarily on the financial details of every project and there was never time to look to the future.

"Guys, we are in this together," said Edward concluding the meeting. "We need to start thinking how we are going to take this company to the next level. I can't do it on my own. Thank you so much for your input and ideas."

As they stood up and left, Joe turned around and said, "Great job boss!"

chapter nine

LEADERSHIFT IN ACTION

The week continued uneventfully, except for an awkward hallway encounter with Joe Palmer late Thursday evening. Joe wanted to thank Edward for the nice gestures concerning his wife and time off, but the two men had held such a comfortable emotional distance for so long that this kind of banter seemed strange. After a moment of studying his shiny shoes, Joe finally mumbled, "Hey, thanks for everything. The family really appreciates it."

Usually articulate, this awkwardness of speech was uncharacteristic for Joe, and Edward was equally uncomfortable.

Still, Joe continued, "If the time off on Friday poses a problem, I can work from the hospital."

Ready to bolt back to his office, Edward quickly retorted, "No, Joe, we'll be fine. Have a good weekend; we got you covered." With that said, he brushed past Joe to the refuge of his office.

So used to getting out of the house early for the Saturday office meeting, that morning, Edward was one of the first parents to arrive at his son's soccer game. Victoria was delighted knowing how happy this would make their eleven-year-old, Eddie. Edward's namesake, the two couldn't appear any different in personality. Playful and outgoing, Eddie wore his heart on his sleeve and was eager to please. He and his dad often clashed, as Eddie's silly antics to gain his dad's attention and affection didn't always go over well with Edward's no-nonsense parenting style. Seeing how well his "fire yourself" approach had gone over with his wife and staff, Edward was eager to gain some cohesiveness in his bewildering relationship with both his son and daughter Hannah.

Edward marveled at the agility and skill of his son on the field, another clear distinction between the two of them. And he lamented all the games he had missed over the years. As he celebrated the team's win with the other friends and family members in the stands, Edward leaned in to inform his wife and Hannah of plans he'd made for Eddie and himself, and he told them to enjoy the rest of their day.

Victoria looked shocked as she nodded in agreement, quickly gathered her belongings, and blew a goodbye kiss at her waving son. Victoria didn't know what to do with herself, but she walked away delighted and sure that she and Hannah would figure it out.

The truth was Edward had no plan at all. The idea popped into his head, and he decided at the spur of the moment to go with it. That had been happening a lot lately.

As an excited Eddie ran over to greet his dad, Edward was at a total loss for what to do with a boy this age. Although Eddie was his son, Edward's unfamiliarity with his likes and dislikes was suddenly dawning on him.

"Dad, did you see that last play? Did you see me? Where's Mom? I saw her leaving, where did she go?" Eddie asked in what seemed like one breath.

"She left to do some girl stuff with Hannah, so I want you to ride with me to deliver toys to some children who don't have as much as we do and who just lost their dad," Edward also said in a single breath, surprised at how quickly the idea came to him.

After agreeing on ice cream first, the two were on their way to the widow's little flat across town. There were some uncomfortable moments of silence during the ride, but soon they began to interview one another. "So, what happened to that work thing you usually do on Saturdays?" Eddie asked slowly, with his head tilted as if the thought had just occurred to him. "Well, I fired myself, son," Edward replied, knowing it'd cause an avalanche of questions. And it did.

The two slowly eased into a fluid banter about everything from soccer, Eddie's friends and teachers, Pablo, and McLand Construction to comic books and superheroes. It was clear from the laughter and learned similarities that they had each made a new friend.

Edward knew in that moment that making amends with his daughter wouldn't be as easy. She was older, a girl and possessed an artist's soul, something totally foreign to her engineer-minded father and mathematical mother. Despite this, he genuinely admired her gift for visual art and couldn't be prouder that his daughter was a rising star at the prestigious Savannah Arts Academy. He knew it was about time he let Hannah know it and work to also build a new relationship with her.

Upon arrival at Mrs. Danford's house, Edward once again didn't have a plan. He knocked on the door as he had weeks earlier. Again, the widow answered with a little one clinging to one leg. He held up the FAO Schwartz bag as if the woman would automatically recognize the name and know what was in it. Of course, she didn't. That wasn't the world in which she lived. The woman looked bewildered and more haggard than before.

Edward began awkwardly. "I took a business trip recently and picked up some toys for the kids. May I?" he said as he motioned to come in.

She stepped to the side, eyeing Edward suspiciously, as the children ran toward him with excitement and anticipation of seeing what this stranger had brought for them.

As he began to take out the toys and dispense them among the three children, Eddie stood in the background and took in the environment, which seemed foreign to him, and observed his father's interaction with the toddlers and five-year-old. So did Mrs. Danford. She observed but didn't quite know what to make of this stranger who seemed to show up at her lowest moments. His first visit found her in early, deep mourning for the loss of her husband. And now, weeks later, the reality of the nightmare had sunk in, and if it weren't for her children and her faith, she might have given up. Her faith wouldn't let her even say the word suicidal, but on this day, she felt it, whether she could bring herself to utter it or not.

Seeing the shiny new toys against the dinginess of her environment and hearing the one thing that could pull her out of despair – the laughter of her children – she began to feel just a glimmer of hope. Her thought was interrupted as she noticed Eddie fingering the wooden cross near the fireplace and the word HOPE.

She smiled with the sudden realization of why this important man would take so much interest in her little family and the problems they faced, especially since his company had been cleared of any wrongdoing.

"Did you come for more prayer, Mr. McLand?" Mrs. Danford asked with the first hint of a smile Edward had seen from her.

The question surprised him. "Sure," he said, looking nervously in Eddie's direction and not quite knowing how to respond. He had fired himself but was still getting accustomed to outward prayer.

As soon as Mrs. Danford grabbed his and his son's hand, Edward also sensed that this was the reason he'd come. He closed his eyes, felt all the love coming from this hurting family and exhaled a deep breath. He then prayed harder than he ever had before, and so did Mrs. Danford. As he was leaving, he held her hand and looked deeply into her sad eyes and said, "It is all going to be OK, trust me, I am working on a plan."

And just like that, they left her world, one of mourning yet of deep spiritual contentment.

chapter ten

A TEST OF LEADERSHIFT

E dward walked into the McLand Construction reception area Monday morning with a new appreciation for his life. He felt grateful and looked around as if seeing everything for the first time. The custom woodwork on the half-moon shaped reception desk, dark hardwood floors and custom-designed wall art was noticed with new appreciation. Michelle's warmth, personal sacrifices and attention to detail in performing her duties as his assistant were appreciated with new intensity. He felt good about himself for the first time in a long time. He almost whistled as he passed Michelle's desk.

"Good morning, Mr. McLand. I just forwarded an email that I think you'll want to look at right away," she said nervously. "Before this morning's leadership meeting."

Edward logged into his computer quickly and began to read an email from the new business prospect threatening to reject McLand Construction's proposal due to the incorrect and incomplete submission of information. Edward slammed his hand on the desk and frantically pushed the button to call Michelle into his office. He held his copy of the Request for Proposal in his right hand up in the air as she entered with a questioning expression on her face. As she hunched her shoulders, she proceeded with caution.

"Well, it appears the section that Joe normally handles had some gaps. We've all been doing a great job covering his workload to accommodate his new Friday schedule, but clearly the team missed something here."

Edward waved Michelle out with a dismissive hand motion and then swiveled his chair in the opposite direction facing the view of downtown Savannah. He was fuming but felt conflicted. Before firing himself, he would have stormed into the Monday morning meeting and roasted Joe for potentially costing him millions. He'd want the entire leadership team to hear as their warning to never make such a costly, embarrassing mistake. The construction world was small, and submitting a shabby proposal was a bad reflection on him as a businessman. Plus, McLand Construction needed this deal more than it had ever needed a project.

Before he could finish his thought, as if on cue, Joe walked in to see if Edward was ready to head to the conference room. Edward sighed deeply.

"What's wrong?" Joe asked, detecting his frustration.

Once again, Edward held the RFP high, and then dramatically let it fall on his desk.

"What's going on with the Low Country Bridge

RFP? That's a done deal I thought," said Joe confused.

Hearing those words infuriated Edward. He could hear his own voice rising as he responded, "I thought so too, Joe, so what the h—" He stopped himself and remembered his last talk with Pablo. He adjusted himself and his tone before beginning again. "There seems to be a problem with section 5.1, and they need us to fix it right away. As soon as the meeting is over, let's go over it together with a fine-toothed comb. I'm sure we can knock this out quickly."

As they walked out together, Edward asked about Joe's wife, and this time he remembered her name. Within two hours of ending the meeting, all the proposal issues had been resolved and the document resubmitted. Edward took a moment to reflect on the height of his emotion, and he shook his head at himself as he realized how connected his esteem was to his professional performance and reputation. He knew he'd definitely have to fire this part of himself.

The sound of his assistant's voice through the intercom startled him. "Edward, the New York developers are requesting a meeting to finalize the deal. Should I make travel arrangements for you and Philip?"

"Yes, but let them know Philip's joining me and that we'll have some amendments to the current contract draft. And please call Allied Taxi's to arrange pick up by Pablo."

The flight was easy, and although the layover in D.C. always felt like an unnecessary nuisance, it allowed Edward to get to know Philip better. He'd worked for McLand six years, and sadly, Edward knew little more than his name. During the hour-long layover, he learned that Philip had been born and raised in New York and started his career on Wall Street before moving to Boston.

Suddenly, Philip's big city-style negotiating savvy made sense to Edward. His wife's family was in Savannah, Georgia, so they chose to relocate there after their second child was born.

Edward thought that Philip was making what would have been a very difficult decision for most successful men sound easy, as he explained why his kids being with the grandparents and his wife's emotional health was more important to him than a rising, lucrative finance career. Edward listened – really listened – and even took mental note that the wife's name was Emily.

Philip also mentioned that their family loved it in Savannah and that the grandparents were a great help since Emily worked as a nurse in the hospital and had crazy hours. Edward was amazed at the complex personal lives his team members were leading right under his nose. He had not been that connected to his own personal story, so, of course, the journey of those around him had eluded him. The process of firing himself was teaching him more every day.

The landing at JFK airport was a smooth one. While Philip seemed to feel at home in the hustle and bustle that met them on the curb of the arrival pick up area, Edward was still uneasy amidst the commotion. He anxiously looked around for Pablo and felt calmed by the familiar smile and handshake, which greeted him moments later.

"Edward, great to see you again, and I see you have a friend this time," Pablo said as he extended a hand to Philip next.

After quick introductions, they were off to the Manhattan office of the developer. Edward was tense about the pending contract discussions and was all business during the ride, as he and Philip rallied to get on the same page for the meeting. Despite his outward calm, Edward was nervous and his confidence had been shaken based on the way earlier negotiations had ended. This was their final opportunity to turn this around and get a decent financial deal for the project. Before even thinking about it, when Edward saw them pull on the street of the office building, he did something he'd never done before when it came to business. Edward said a quick, silent prayer. He waved a goodbye to Pablo, and they disappeared into the building. Pablo noticed the prayer, smiled and then said one himself.

At the end of the day, Pablo was surprised to see Edward alone and even more surprised to see his child-like exuberance. Edward was very pleased with how the contract signing had gone.

Philip was masterful in the way he handled the developers, and the contract amendments were restructured so fairly to both sides that it left little room for argument. He had complained so much about the slick Yankees and had no idea that he had a Yankee on his team who could go toe to toe with them. He knew team diversity was important for HR and political correctness, but his eyes were opening to how all the different backgrounds, cultures, and experiences of his staff really did individually bring something valuable to the table and ultimately impact the bottom line. They had reworked the contract with a performance bonus clause for early completion of certain phases that would hopefully lead to a profitable project for McLand Construction. Edward was happy, to say the least.

"It was a good day I take it?" Pablo asked looking through the rearview mirror.

"Yes, excellent! I've made dinner arrangements with another prospective developer and have a few hours until we meet. Central Park was nice last time. Let's head back there," replied Edward.

With his job done, Philip had headed to the airport earlier, as Edward waited for the final contract to be revised and printed for signatures.

"Central Park it is," Pablo said with a wide grin. He too couldn't contain his elation as he noticed the marked difference in Edward.

chapter eleven

PURPOSE

As they found the perfect stone to rest on at the park, Edward couldn't wait to share details of his moment during the bumpy plane ride with Pablo and how he had fired himself and all that had transpired in the weeks since they last saw each other. Pablo listened intently and was very pleased that Edward had finally reached a place of understanding. He was also sad that soon there wouldn't be much more he could teach his new, unlikely friend.

When Edward was finished, Pablo said pensively, "One of my favorite scriptures in the Bible found in Romans says, 'We know that in all things God works for the good of those who love him, who have been called according to his purpose.' It sounds to me like you have discovered your purpose. How awesome, Edward!"

Edward had come a long way, but the riddles in which Pablo spoke still slightly irritated him, especially at a moment like this where it should be all about celebration. He'd grown to know that the lessons were always worth a little extra patience on his part. Still, he couldn't imagine what purpose had to do with anything he had just shared or how his business operated. Truth be told, he didn't quite even know what it meant.

Pablo continued. "It is widely known that companies that have a clear vision as to why they exist and what makes them uniquely different succeed at greater levels than those who do not. So purpose then becomes the reason as to why the company is in business. Purpose is accomplished by establishing some very fundamental guidelines that serve to align everyone and every decision in the same direction. First and foremost, a company must have a Mission Statement that is simple but captures the essence of what the company does, how they do it, why they do it and for whom it is done."

"But before you put together a Mission Statement, you and your leaders must understand the 'why' of your existence," Pablo continued, "hugely successful companies and individuals that understand why they are in business and why they do what they do will outperform those that do not. And if you think that you are in this to make money, you are missing the most fundamental element of liberating and successful organizations. Edward, everyone in the construction business knows the what and the how of the business. The what is that they build stuff and the how is that they follow someone's design and instructions. The question to you is, why do you do that?"

Edward watched a flock of birds congregate near his and Pablo's feet as they had done on the last visit to the park. The feel of the wind on his skin, and the sound of birds' chirping together with the varied sounds of the park made a medley that caused Edward to involuntarily close his eyes and tilt his head back slightly. Pablo's soothing tone and the wisdom with which spoke was also melodic to Edward. Everything that Pablo said made perfect sense, yet Edward still had to resist the urge to dismiss his advice as less than valid because he was, after all, just a taxi driver. "How does he know so much and why do I feel so compelled to listen?" Edward questioned inwardly while concurrently chastising himself for having the thought.

"Edward, most managers and leaders in organizations are good tactical thinkers and excellent problem solvers. What makes the difference in great organizations, are leaders that are also visionaries and have a deep understanding of a purpose that goes beyond the obvious. And they understand this in their personal life as well; they are not mutually exclusive."

Pablo let that statement sink in for a minute before he proceeded.

"There are many individuals in this world that are materially wealthy and have certain powers and at the same time are not happy; they are not content. The concept of success eludes them, and there is a need for more – more power, more wealth, more recognition, more, more, more. Edward, the secret of success lies within ourselves; continually working towards a worthy cause that brings contentment to the soul while being significant to others and influencing the world around you in a positive and everlasting way."

Pablo stopped talking as he contemplated his surroundings.

Edward noticed Pablo was deep in thought and gazing at a vibrant cardinal that had joined the increasing number of birds around them. "Pablo that is some heavy stuff you are talking about. The why is something I am going to need to get back to you later because I do not have an answer for you right this second. Mission statements are the norm, I know, but don't you agree they can be useless for many companies. Just a bunch of words with little meaning to anyone except the dinosaurs who created them," said Edward, shaking his head.

"Mission statements vary widely from company to company. If you look at the mission statements of Fortune 500 companies, it is clear that there is not a universally accepted way of making one. The reason a company exists is not something that should have to be memorized or frozen in frames that employees have long stopped noticing," Pablo responded. "The mission statement is your North Star; it should reveal internally and externally what the organization values and should align the principles and motivations in one or two sentences. Basically, if you have to memorize it, then it is probably not authentic and descriptive of what you do, how you do it and for whom you do it. In short, a Mission Statement is your identity!"

"Not to be confused with a Vision Statement," said Pablo, "this mission statement is then supported by a set of guiding principles that are based on the company's core values. These guiding principles vary depending on industry but most companies will include employee respect and trust, safety, training the employees, environment, customer satisfaction, quality, continuous improvement, profitability etc."

Edward replied thoughtfully, "So the mission statement and the guiding principles should serve as the foundation for big picture decision-making and will guide the company's strategy?"

"Exactly!" Pablo replied. "If you say that you are committed to training the workforce and then do not put the resources in place to do so, then you are not walking the talk. Likewise, if you say that you are committed to continuous improvement and then do not put processes in place like Lean and Six Sigma, you are not committed to continuous improvement. The Vision Statement is aspirational and futuristic in nature; it is the overarching goal of what you want to become."

"I see," said Edward. "Then at McLand Construction, the Vision Statement will be to 'Become the premier construction company in the Southeast.' And I guess we will need to identify what the word premier means and how to track if we are moving in that direction."

"Yes, and once you establish the Mission Statement, Guiding Principles and the Vision Statement, then the company can work on its strategy, basically setting long-term and short-term goals," Pablo agreed.

Pablo continued, "The planning for these goals starts from the outside in. In other words, you need to know where you want to be in five years so that you can set where you need to be in three years to meet the five-year goals. So then you need to know what you need to do the next twelve months to track in the direction of the three-year goals. You understand?"

"I think so," Edward replied. "So the Vision Statement is like setting the coordinates in your sailboat's GPS when you are going on a long journey. The boat will get off course by the wind, the weather, or mechanical issues, but with the coordinates in place, you can always get back on course!"

"Now you're getting it!" Pablo exclaimed. "Regardless of size, companies without a Vision Statement and long and short-term goals, are like a sailboat without a rudder; more often than not, they cannot get out of the port to embark on the journey."

Pablo continued, "In order to create long and short-term goals, they must have a strategy, a very definite plan, on how you are going to get there. For most companies, especially publicly traded ones, the goal and strategy are to make money for the investors, it is creating shareholder equity. It is the reason they exist. Companies today are looking for other reasons that are equally as important as making money. These reasons are referred to as institutional logic or social logic, and they can run parallel to economic logic, which boils down to financial health and being profitable. In other words, companies are looking at how its decisions are impacting its culture, the customers it serves, the community in which it serves and the environment in which we all live. The latest generation, the millennials, are demanding that their employers look at these other reasons. It is part of a larger purpose and the reason they would want to remain working for a company."

Edward nodded in agreement, thinking of the shift he had been noticing in the business arena and how green principles and achieving some form of LEED certification had become the standard in just about every project they had built in the last few years.

"Absolutely, there are a number of things companies are doing such as zero carbon footprint, flexible hours for employees, wellness programs and other innovative initiatives. I think you've helped me better understand," said Pablo. "OK, here is where it gets a little more complicated. The same way that companies need this framework for their success, so will you.

"Edward, you need to know why you get out of bed every morning, what gets you on the balls of your feet and drives you through life. Hopefully, it is more than just building a construction company and making money. You need to understand the motive behind your life and whether you are going to be significant in this world, or are you going to be like most people who go through life punching a card and moving and breathing without a purpose or a mission. Edward, I know your heart. You have within you the power and the will to be different and create something really special; a world of love and trust, a world of contentment and peace, a world of service and giving. You can make this a better place for you, your family, your friends, your people and your community; I know you have the energy and the drive, it just needs to be directed in the right path. Pray and follow your heart, and everything else will come together; of that I am certain!"

chapter twelve

DISCIPLINE

Having gotten restless sitting, the two men walked until they found another resting spot. Right away, Edward noticed the tiny colony of ants near them. He watched as one appeared to be carrying a little tiny piece of food hurriedly to some unknown destination.

"Well, it sounds like McLand is off to a decent start with our understanding of where we want to go and our vision of what we want to become, but it sounds like we still have some work to do," said Edward.

"Absolutely, and that work will start with you, Edward," Pablo replied. "Once you have committed to lead by serving and caring and are actually putting those values into practice, you can then create alignment with everyone regarding McLand's future direction. The key component of success will be bridging the plan with execution, and that's where discipline comes in.

Discipline at its core is consistent performance of the agreed upon plan and having a system in place to hold everyone accountable for desired results. When a culture of discipline is weaved in the fabric of the organization, high performance outcomes become natural and anticipated."

Edward chuckled watching the highly disciplined actions of the ants gathering food. "Yeah, looks like these guys have the right idea," he said pointing toward the colony.

Pablo smiled and nodded in agreement. "Do you know who else has the right idea about discipline's connection to success?" he questioned. "Successful athletes, like high performing companies, understand that success comes from a disciplined dedication to carefully planning every action, every move, and every strategy over and over again until it becomes natural, instinctive and effortless. Greatness is then achieved when this discipline of planning converges with God's given gifts and a passion for excellence."

Edward looked confused and still carried remnants of defensiveness. He turned his gaze from the ants to Pablo and held up a hand in protest. "Pablo, it's not that deep. I've been in business for years and executing is simply sticking with the plan. Plainly put, it is not giving in to the temptation of quitting or deferring from the plan. Execution is to make it happen!" Edward said authoritatively as if Pablo could hear his mental plea for Pablo to stop talking in riddles.

"Paul writes about it in the Book of Hebrews," said Pablo, "when he says 'let us throw off everything that hinders and the sin that so easily entangles, and let us run with perseverance the race marked out for us'."

Edward continued as if Pablo hadn't said a word.

"Execution is running past our first wind into our second. It is not giving up when the odds are against us; it is staying focused on the work at hand. The great basketball coach Jim Valvano, whose legacy continues although he died of cancer many years ago, said in his famous speech, 'Never, ever give up!'"

Pablo noted the far away but determined look in Edward's eyes. "You're right, my friend, it takes discipline to stay engaged, to stay connected with the task at hand and to consistently deliver on the goals. The winds of this world will blow you off course, but it is determination and purpose that will bring you back," Pablo said now with a far away, reminiscent look in his own eyes.

He snapped back to reality and continued, "With the same enthusiasm you execute on your plan, you then must measure the progress being made. Regardless of what the task is. If you do not measure, you won't know if you are on track. It is a weakness of many leaders and organizations to become complacent, lazy, and undisciplined. Having performance indicators allows you to then determine if your employees are leading and executing to their potential. Measuring is caring and measuring is essential for personal development, growth and wise decision-making. Unless you have a goal to benchmark performance against, you will be like a plane flying through the clouds, not knowing where the next mountain will be," Pablo said letting his eyes float toward the clear sky and pure white clouds.

Edward looked toward the clouds too. Feeling more relaxed in the conversation, he replied, "I get it, Pablo, but you're preaching to the choir. If I weren't disciplined, I couldn't have built a company as successful as McLand, but getting my employees to adapt the same work ethic isn't as easy as you make it sound." Edward glanced quickly at his watch. They stood in synchrony, then walked toward the curb as Pablo began to speak again.

"We live in a world that is moving and changing faster than any other time in history. The global connectivity has removed barriers that once seemed inconceivable. I know all too well that not being disciplined and focused with a commitment to measuring results along the way will relegate an organization to mediocrity or just average," said Pablo evoking a strange look from Edward.

Edward wondered how this taxi driver would know these things, but he emphatically nodded in agreement.

"And, to stay ahead of the curve and the competition, we must constantly improve on what we are doing. We can't assume that just because it is working, it always will. There are hundreds of companies that are no longer in business because they did not improve, innovate or remain disciplined enough to invest in research and development," Edward said as if he were talking to the air, rather than the man walking next to him.

Pablo added, "Never stop talking to your customers or looking at trends clearly staring you in the face. You must have a commitment to continuous improvement and a process for gathering customer feedback. Also, implement systems such as Lean and Six Sigma that will help you identify gaps, reduce waste, improve efficiencies, speed to market and improve quality in all you do.

"And one last thing about discipline Edward, you must also implement that concept in your personal life. We can easily get caught up with work and forget to live a balanced life. I am not saying that the work/life balance concept is a static one. In fact, seldom will the three circles of your work, your family and your self will be balanced. Life is dynamic and unpredictable, but you should always tweak the journey towards balance, and that my friend requires serious discipline."

The ride back to the hotel was silent, as both men contemplated the conversation.

Edward was anxious to get back and implement some changes at McLand Construction. He silently wondered how his friend Pablo planned to utilize all the valuable business knowledge he'd just shared with him in his own life. Maybe he could find a place for Pablo at McLand. Before he could wonder any further, he had reached his destination, and it was time to exit the taxi.

Edward took a mental note to reach back out to Pablo to extend a job offer. Anyone with his level of knowledge should be putting it to better use, he thought. But first he had a few things to put in order at McLand.

"Please pick me up at 6:30 tomorrow morning, my flight is not until noon, but I am anxious to get back and hope I can catch an earlier flight."

"No problem," said Pablo, "there is one more topic I can share with you on the way to the airport."

"Alright Pablo, what is it? You are not going to leave me hanging are you?"

"Well before you get back and start making changes, you need to create a strategy for your business. There are hundreds of books on strategy and leaders who teach it. I will share with you a simple, yet effective process. It's been a long day my friend. Get some rest, and I'll see you bright and early."

chapter thirteen

STRATEGY

As Pablo's taxi arrived, Edward was already outside anxiously waiting. He had a hard time sleeping the night before; there was so much information floating around in his head. As always, even when he didn't get enough sleep, he was up around five ready for the first cup of coffee. He was a morning person; he called that time "Edward time". That hour or so when the world slept, and he was up with his thoughts, planning the day or reading a book. He could not possibly understand how people could get up in the morning rushing to take a shower, grabbing breakfast on the way out the door and fighting traffic to work. Basically, being stressed out before sitting at their desks! He preferred a smooth and easy morning routine, two cups of coffee minimum before getting in the shower. All this before Victoria or the kids woke up. He had been doing it since college.

"Good morning," said Pablo cheerfully, "I see you are ready to roll."

"Buenos dias Pablo," replied Edward with a bit of a chuckle, "I've been up learning Spanish. Perhaps one day you will teach me – nahh, I am too old to learn, this old dog couldn't learn that trick. I am, however, encouraging my kids to learn it. There is a strong Hispanic community in our city."

"Well, I heard it mentioned that if you are not related to a Hispanic now, you will be in 20 years!"

"I believe that," said Edward, "there is a huge influx of immigrants in our schools. Good people."

"Alright Edward, grab some paper and something to write with. We have thirty minutes to the airport, and it is important you take notes on what I am going to share with you. This can take a few hours to explain, so I will give you the highlights. I am talking about strategic planning, which is nothing more than creating a high level plan that will allow you and McLand to reach your long and short- term goals."

"Hold on Pablo, we do goal setting every year. I get together with my senior managers and we spend a day in a conference room of one of the local hotels and we hammer out the goals for the following year; been doing it for years."

"And how has your performance been?" asked Pablo incredulous.

"All over the place. We typically see how things are going at the time and the mood of the business climate to project next year's goals."

"Hmm, you and most companies. OK, let me help you here; you have to do some serious homework before you get behind closed doors; otherwise, it is like shooting in the dark. You got a pad and pen out?"

"OK, shoot," said Edward, sounding a bit skeptical.

"I can't see what you are doing, but let me start with an illustration, a graphical representation. Set the paper length wise and draw a box next to the left margin and one next to the right margin. Now draw three larger boxes on top of each other in the middle of the page. Got it?"

"Sure, sure."

"Write on the left box the following, Purpose, Mission, Vision and Guiding Principles and write on the right box Long-Term Goals and Short-Term Goals. Clearly before you even get started on strategic planning you must have defined the items in the left box. We've already talked about this – don't waste your time going through this if your goals do not start and align with your mission and vision."

"Alright, I got that. What about the three boxes in the middle?"

"That's the homework you must do before the meeting. Write on the top box Organizational Profile, Strategic Analysis in the middle and Business Intelligence in the bottom one. I can do a dissertation on this, but I will keep it simple and to the point."

"Keep going," said Edward.

"Now add four bullets in each of the boxes. Here we go. In the top box write down people, structure, clients and operations. These four go in the middle box: competitive analysis, economic analysis, environmental forecast, and industry trends. And write the following in the bottom box: economic logic, brand awareness, innovation and growth. Got all that?"

"I have," replied Edward, "this is a lot of information; what does it all mean?"

"You are right; this is more than you can absorb in the cab ride to the airport. Just write it down, and then you can percolate it later on the plane and do some research on your own. I am going to give you a statement for each of the points, and you can then work on each statement and put it all together. I promise you that it will all make sense at the end. Here we go:

People – who do you have, who do you need to

replace, and who do you need to hire to take you to the next level?

Structure – is the company properly structured with a well established line of command or is their confusion of accountability? Everyone should have one person they report to.

Clients – analyze your customer list and make sure you are spending an appropriate amount of time with those who keep you in business. Reduce the list if you need to.

Operations – are you operating lean and efficiently with an appropriate enterprise system in place with integrated data and communication?

Competitive analysis – do you know your market share and do you have an understanding of your rivals? This can get pretty extensive if you do a full competitive analysis that includes substitutes, barriers to entry, switching costs and the competitive influential forces of your customers and suppliers. We'll leave this conversation for another day.

Economic analysis – what are the economists saying about your industry growth trend in your region?

Environmental forecast – what is happening around you that is out of your control and will impact your business?

Industry trends – what is changing in your industry that you need to be aware of and requires that you be ready for, such as new procurement processes or technology?

Economic logic – you probably have this one figured out, but it is essential that you and your managers know your numbers and your margins.

Brand awareness – are you articulating your brand in the market place and are you differentiating yourself from the competition? What is your brand promise?

Innovation – do you think about looking at ways to get better and do you have an innovation strategy in place?

Growth – what are your growth plans? Are you adding new services, are you expanding your existing offering or are you going to grow geographically?"

"OK, how do I go about getting all this information? Man, there is no way I can to do it myself!" cried Edward.

"This is where you delegate to your managers. Go through this list and assign responsibilities to each of them; let them do the research and own the data, there is a tremendous amount of information on the web. Here, call Doug. He can help you with the first box," said Pablo as he handed Edward a business card.

They pulled into the departure terminal, and this time Pablo got out of the cab and gave Edward a strong and warm hug.

"Thanks Pablo, you have been like an angel. I can't wait for my family to meet you. I will definitely bring them to New York on the next trip."

"Great, I look forward to meeting them. Take care my friend. Vaya con Dios."

chapter fourteen

16 MONTHS LATER

The Call

Edward was in the kitchen cutting up tomatoes, mushrooms, peppers and onions. He'd whipped a dozen eggs and was ready to start his morning routine with the family. He had become Chef Edward, fixing breakfast for Victoria and the kids every morning. He loved it. Instead of getting ready and leaving to work before they were up as he used to, Edward now would sit down with his family and enjoy an intimate breakfast with them. What a great way to start the day!

As hard as they tried, Hannah was always running behind; being a fifteen-year-old getting ready every morning to face the world was complicated. That was her standard line for being late. Edward and Victoria stopped arguing with her about it; it was a losing battle.

"Vickie, what's your day like?" asked Edward. His standard question every morning.

"Glad you asked, I have a meeting at the Savannah School of Art and Design with a counselor. I mentioned it to you last week; I am considering taking a couple of art courses next semester, but Eddie needs to be across town for soccer trials, you know the new challenge league that starts next month. Can you take him? If you are too busy I will reschedule my meeting, just totally spaced out about soccer."

Edward reached for his phone and looked at his schedule. I have a meeting later this afternoon, but I will get Joe to cover for me, and if he can't, I am sure I will find someone who can. You go ahead to your meeting at SCAD; I am anxious to find out what they think of this move. It will certainly change things around here!"

The conversation was lively as everyone finished the omelets and toast.

"Hannah, I know you hate this, but sorry sweetie, it is your morning to clean up and put the plates in the dishwasher," said Edward with a grin across his face.

"Got to run, we have our monthly staff meeting at work this morning."

It was a twenty-minute ride to the office; a time that Edward used to reflect and start planning the day. Today was different. His thoughts wondered in a different direction. He contemplated his life and how much had transpired since he met Pablo a year and a half ago in New York on a taxi cab ride to the airport. Prior to that encounter, he would have chalked it up to luck and coincidence. Today, he saw it as part of a larger purpose in his life; he thought to himself, you can't make this stuff up.

He had promised Pablo that he would bring his family to meet him, and he had promised his kids he would take them to New York this year. Something that was uncharacteristic of Edward to take the lead in planning a family vacation. This was something that Victoria had always taken care of. He made a mental note to call Pablo when he got in and plan a trip for the following weekend. The kids were off for Columbus Day and New York would be great in October.

His thought shifted to Victoria and how fortunate he felt that she took him back. The divorce papers were burnt during a renewal of vows celebrations about a year ago. He was madly in love with her and already looking forward to their weekly Monday lunch date - today.

Monday was a day that Edward was typically in the office, so he had made it a point not to schedule a business lunch that day. This weekly get together, which included a scheduled lunch and dinner date, had served to connect them like never before. At first, these commitments seemed a bit like a chore, but Edward began to engage his wife in his business dealings and would usually ask her opinion about complicated matters. They had met when they were young. He was studying

Civil Engineering when he met her at a Georgia versus Georgia Tech game in Athens, Georgia, where she was studying to be a math teacher. He was immediately smitten with her looks and her personality. It took some work and many trips between Atlanta and Athens until she finally decided to go out with him.

Victoria always had practical advice. She was smart, logical and had a tender heart, with a love for people that came to her naturally.

She balanced him and also loved him with all of his imperfections. He knew that.

His mind then drifted to the staff meeting this morning, but focused on the ways they were currently serving the community.

The company had committed to align itself with a non-profit organization and encouraged the employees to participate. It made sense that being in the construction industry, they would choose an organization that built houses for the poor. It had been a great success with almost everyone participating in the last two projects. Even Edward showed up with his family.

The kids set up a lemonade stand and gave out free ice-cold glasses of lemonade to the group. Eddie, already showing signs of a future entrepreneur, wanted to charge a dollar a cup but lost that battle. His father instead, helped him build a lemonade stand he would set up every Saturday morning near a greenway trail close to their house; it was a thriving business!

Edward was also looking forward to Friday. It was the second annual Bill Danford Memorial Golf Tournament at Forsyth Park. McLand Construction was the corporate sponsor and had committed to two foursomes as well as sponsoring one of the par threes. Last year, they had a dozen foursomes, and this year they were expecting to field enough players to fill one of the courses for the shotgun start. They were planning to grow so that all three courses would be needed. The fire department had done a great job getting the word out, as well as Edward who chaired the organizing committee. All the proceeds were split between a college fund set up for Bill's three kids and support for his widow's day-to-day living expenses.

With that last thought, Edward pulled into his company's parking lot and finally found a parking space a couple of rows from the main entrance. Gone was the "Reserved for CEO" sign next to the building.

Edward went straight to his office after greeting everyone with warm good mornings. He quickly sat at his computer and checked flights for next Friday evening coming back Monday afternoon.

He had not been back to New York since his last encounter with Pablo and was looking forward to getting back to Central Park, this time with Victoria and his two kids.

He still wanted to find out about Pablo's background. There were so many questions he wanted to ask this mysterious man. It seemed every time he thought to ask, Pablo would cut him off and share another incredible insight.

Edward also couldn't wait to share the amazing progress the company was making, all the initiatives they had started and his rekindled relationship with his wife and kids. But most importantly, he wanted to share his continued personal growth and how firing himself as his own Higher Power had completely transformed his life. And it was all thanks to him.

Edward decided to do just that. Rather than asking his assistant, he called Allied Cab Company directly.

"Allied Taxi Service, how may I direct your call?" the woman who answered said, half singing.

Edward asked if he could speak with one of the taxi drivers, Pablo Cervantes. To his astonishment, the woman paused only a moment before saying matter-of-factly that Pablo was gone. He had left about six months ago without saying a word or indicating where he was going. They really missed him as he was such a nice and gentle person.

"Sir, more than a dozen different people have called in the past six months asking for this same driver. I have been working here for 20 years, and I assure you that we have never had anyone just leave and disappear the way he has," she said with sadness in her voice.

Edward replied, speaking partly to himself, "No, it's not possible." He held the phone with the woman's words echoing in his ears. The past six months, he thought. He wondered how that could be possible when he had just been a passenger in Pablo's car less than a year and a half earlier. He and the dozen other people who had called looking for Pablo couldn't all be insane could they?

"There must be some mistake," he said still shaking his head with curiosity and disbelief.

Sounding exasperated this time, the lady responded abruptly with a heavier New York accent. "Look pal, if you and all the others who keep calling can tell me where to find Pablo, I'll go and drag him here myself. Especially since all of you keep refusing the other drivers I offer." She let out a deep sigh as if it came with a prayer that the person on the other end would finally get it. "For the last time, Pablo Cervantes worked for Allied but is now gone, but do me a favor and pray that he walks through these doors one day soon."

Without a word, Edward slowly replaced the phone in its cradle, bowed his head and did just that.

chapter fifteen

SAN FRANCISCO

Grace slams the glass door as she exits the building on Geary Street. Phone to her ear and a leather briefcase hanging from her shoulder, she is irate, yelling on the phone and ready for battle. It is a cold typical midday in the Bay area with tourists and business people intermingling as they go about their lives in this fast pace city. Not quite New York, just a different kind of rhythm and flow.

Grace is slender, tall, and attractive dressed in a perfectly fitting and matching business pant and suit. She has just finished a meeting with the bank and things did not go well.

She sees a parked taxi cab and without hesitation opens the cab door and slides into the back seat not missing a beat in her phone conversation. After a few seconds, she gets desperate and taps on the glass divider to get the driver's attention.

The man turns around and in a soothing voice asks, "Where to ma'am?"

"To the airport," she replies curtly and immediately gets back to berating the person on the other end of the phone.

As he drives away, Pablo smiles and whispers to himself, "I caught another one!"

Afterword

The Monthly Staff Meeting

Sean had just finished giving his monthly report. It was the first day of the month and the entire staff, except for the field crews, was gathered in the large cafe that had just been recently renovated with the latest technology, including video conferencing. He went through the progress of the mixed-used development project being developed by the "guys in suits" from New York. The project was being fast-tracked with the rough grading already being done and most of the foundations already poured. The project consisted of four five-story buildings with retail on the ground floor, offices on the second floor and condos on the upper three levels. There were several out parcels where other contractors were busy building a Starbucks, Panera Bread, a couple of trendy restaurants, a Verizon store and what would be the largest workout facility in Savannah. Sean had reported that the favorable weather had helped the crew move ahead of schedule, which would trigger the quarterly performance bonuses Philip negotiated into the contract.

Edward sat in the back of the room allowing Joe to run the meeting, feeling a deep sense of satisfaction watching a high performance organization at work. It hadn't always been this way.

Len, the chief estimator, was next and announced by ringing the bell located at the entrance to the cafe, that they had just been awarded the new $30 million research and lab facility at Georgia Southern University in Statesboro, about 50 miles away. It was a significant win since it was one of their major goals this year. After focusing on the private sector for the last decade, a decision to diversify into the institutional and municipal markets had been made at their strategic planning session six months earlier. Everyone present clapped and cheered as Len gave the credit to Brad and Tim for their diligent work in identifying certain value engineering changes that saved the university a little over one million dollars without reducing the square footage or compromising the architectural vernacular of the building. Their innovative and creative approach to staging the project, scheduling the multiple subs and cutting three months from the proposed schedule gave McLand the lead in the negotiation and ultimately the contract.

Mauricio was next with a stellar report on the company's safety record. They had gone the last eight months without a reportable injury or a loss time accident. Safety had always been important at McLand, but since the building fire a year and a half ago, the company had set safety as its number one priority. In fact, their number one guiding principle was "Safety without compromise."

He also reported that the monthly training workshops and the toolbox talks had been going right on schedule as he proudly showed on the screen the spreadsheet outlining every workshop with the names of those who had attended. The company had instituted a peer-to-peer safety awareness program that compensated participants with a small gift anytime someone made a colleague aware of a safety violation. There was push back at first, but once it was understood that this was in the best interest of the team and company, everyone started looking out for their teammates' well-being.

Janet followed with an outline of several company policy changes regarding health care benefits. Going forward, the company would start paying for thirty percent of all family health insurance benefits with the goal to increase the coverage to fifty percent by the end of the following year. Once again, this tracked with one of the three-year goals established at the strategic planning session. She also announced that the second cycle of workshop conferences for new employees and those who missed the first cycle, was scheduled to start the second Thursday of the next month. These conferences covered recruiting the best talent, understanding behavior, training the trainer, manage- ment tools, emotional intelligence, motivation and team building, and introduction to continuous improvement using Lean principles.

Philip presented the company's financials. Edward had always kept this information very close to his chest. Since starting the company, the only person who also knew the numbers was the controller. He decided previously during the strategic planning session that to get buy in, from everyone, full operational transparency was necessary. Everyone needed to know how the company was doing financially. He had been afraid to let anyone know when it had been a good year because he figured everyone would be asking for a raise. Or when McLand didn't do well, he felt as if it would look bad on him personally. With his renewed love for the team, he committed to share generously, and at the same time, Edward expected everyone to perform at their best. It was working.

Joe finished the meeting by announcing that Philip's baby boy had been born the week before and both mom and son were doing well.

Edward was filled with joy and proud of himself for knowing why this was such a miraculous moment for his employee. He also mentioned that Chris, an assistant project manager, was leaving to spend a month in Kenya as part of a church group that was going to build a well and teach a local village how to use the water using some very innovative gardening techniques that would yield more than twice the quantity they were currently growing. Lastly, the name of those having birthdays that month appeared on the screen, and everyone was reminded that the birthday pizza lunch was coming that Thursday.

Joe closed off the monthly meeting with a huge smile and a "have a great month" statement. As everyone filed out, several came by to thank Edward for the new healthcare initiative and the huge difference that was going to make in their lives. He had never felt prouder of his team. They had been there all along. He just had not taken the time to notice. He would never have fathomed spending an hour of "production time" in a company-wide meeting. He shuddered at how short-sighted he had been.

Just as Sean was exiting the room, Edward reminded him that they had a one-on-one meeting at eleven that morning.

The One-on-One

Edward had learned to schedule a one-on-one every month with his direct reports, which consisted of Sean, construction operations manager; Len, chief estimator; Philip, financial controller; Mauricio, safety manager; Janet, human resources manager; and Joe, director of marketing and business development. These one-on-one meetings were a major priority for everyone and had been placed on the calendar every month for the next year. Everyone understood that there had to be a major reason for canceling or re-scheduling this meeting. Edward, who in the past would blow-off personnel meetings, had disciplined himself never to schedule anything that would compromise these meetings. His assistant was also well aware of it.

The one-on-one meetings lasted 45 minutes to an hour, and they followed a specific agenda, depending on that person's role in the company. Each of Edward's direct reports had five key performance indicators for which they were responsible. These KPIs were like gauges on the dashboard of a car and served to guide performance and accountability. In addition to reviewing the KPIs and measuring how they were tracking on pre-established goals and objectives, Edward would review and help his managers set both business and personal monthly goals, as well as review how they were tracking towards their yearly goals.

At the beginning, this was very difficult for both Edward and his managers. For someone who had been completely disengaged from his employees' personal lives, he was now holding them accountable for achieving both personal and business goals. Usually, the personal goals related to going to the gym, participating in events, taking the spouse out on dates, spending time with their kids and planning vacations. As the months progressed, his direct reports looked forward to sharing their progress and letting Edward know how their family lives had improved by setting specific goals to spend quality time with those they loved.

The one-on-one meeting elevated the sense of mutual trust to another level. This had helped his direct reports feel more confident in team meetings and more trusting in others in the organization. In fact, it was a mandate that they hold similar one-on-one meetings with their direct reports. This intimate business communication had dramatically increased morale, performance and accountability throughout the entire company.

The OHI

Edward was reminded by his assistant that Doug Buckner, his mentor and coach, was coming over after lunch to share the results of the latest Organizational Health Index (OHI), which they were going to review and compare to the one the company had taken twelve months earlier. The anticipation was killing him.

Over lunch, he discussed with Victoria his upcoming meeting with Doug and how they both enjoyed being able to measure progress in real numbers. One of the reasons Edward engaged Doug over a year ago was to help him change the culture of McLand Construction.

When Edward arrived back at his office, Doug was already there waiting. He had arrived ten minutes earlier as was his custom. He was once taught many years ago that there were three main points to getting referred in business, in addition to doing a good job. First, always be on time as it showed your client that you respect the value of his time; second, always be polite by saying please and thank you, regardless of the circumstances or mood one was in, and lastly, do what you said you were going to do and finish it within the timeframe you committed.

Edward had known Doug since school when they were classmates studying civil engineering. After graduating with a Masters' degree in structural engineering, Doug worked for a couple of consulting firms and finally started his own company back in his hometown of Savannah. He grew the practice into one of the top engineering firms in the Southeast with offices in Atlanta, Raleigh, and Orlando.

Doug was a visionary always looking to improve on processes and systems. Several years ago, he decided to take everything he had developed at his company and share it with leaders of other companies. His engineering background helped him tremendously as he was immediately in demand for his innovative approach to his management consulting business. Nothing was left to chance, as he measured everything. He developed the Organizational Health Index, which he administered at the beginning of the engagement and then twelve to sixteen months later. On an average, his clients saw a twenty percent improvement in the overall score.

The Results

Doug, I hope I didn't keep you waiting," said Edward as he rushed through the front door of the office. "I just finished having lunch with Victoria and got carried away discussing what you are about to share with me. You know how she loves numbers."

"Edward, I am so happy to know you are continuing your Monday lunches with her. Are you still doing a weekly date night?" asked Doug, who helped Edward come to terms with these commitments.

"I am not allowed to miss those for the world! The times I've had to be out of town, I had to reschedule, and believe me, it never bodes well when that happens. What I have learned is that we are our own worst enemy by allowing trivial stuff to creep in and take over our lives. Once we decided that it was more important to spend quality time together on Wednesday night and Friday night with the kids, as well as observing Sunday with church activities, some of the other issues just kind of vanished. Enough about that!

I am anxious to find out the numbers of the OHI and the Servant Leadership Survey," said Edward enthusiastically. "Let's see what kind of progress we have made."

He ushered Doug to the conference room. He had made it a habit over the last year to have meetings in the conference room instead of his office, which felt more neutral and less threatening.

"Edward, I am very impressed with what you have done with your company over the past year. There is still room for improvement, but frankly, I wasn't sure if you could move the needle the way you desired. Here, let me pull out both reports, and I can go over the highlights before I give you your new OHI number and the improvements made in the Servant Leadership Survey."

"Come on Doug. You are going to make me wait? You know I like to get to the bottom line first. Let's discuss the servant leadership survey first," said Edward.

"If you recall, we decided to administer that survey to just the managers which included the leadership team, the project managers, and the second tier managers. I think we should have everyone in the company take this survey. As a reminder, this survey has 20 questions on a scale from 1 to 5 and it is a confidential assessment; I would think, though, that your leaders would want to share their results with the team. As far as your results, you made a significant improvement going from an average score of 2.6 to 3.9. As you know, in your case, we also asked your leadership team to rate you using the same survey, and their overall composite rated at 3.6, up from the initial one of 2.2, so you were not that far off in both cases. As you can see, there were only three areas where you rated a bit higher than what your team thought. See here in the question about humility, you gave yourself a 3 but most everyone rated you a 2, which is a marked improvement from last time when the average of the question was a 1.5, and likewise with the question about patience. Once again, you rated yourself much higher than your team's perception."

Edward looked a bit disappointed. He had been working so hard at thinking before acting and trying to filter his thoughts before reacting. But yes, there had been occasions when his former self showed his ugly face. The times that happened were now fewer and farther apart. There was still so much work to do in this area. He had taken a couple of behavioral assessments, and it was clear that his controlling behavioral dimensions were high assertiveness and low patience. Basically, he battled with a ready-shoot-aim kind of behavior. The good news was that the number was trending upward, and with more supernatural help and guidance, he knew that they would continue in that direction.

"The overall average for those taking the servant leadership assessment showed a marked improvement from a year ago. Edward, these are significant gains in just one year. If you stay focused on the things that matter to your people and continue to build teams where everyone trusts each other, you will hit your three-year goal. I overheard your receptionist discussing the new healthcare benefits and other great things you are implementing. Let's wait about six months and then we will send this survey to everyone in the company; having it online will make it easy for all your employees to take it."

"Good, I am pleased, and yes I know there is plenty of room for improvement. I guess, there will always be room for improvement when it comes to being a servant leader; humbleness, humility, patience, kindness, gentleness and forgiveness, the fruit of the Spirit, just do not come natural to most people, including me."

Doug nodded. "Let's talk about the Organizational Health Index results. A quick overview of what this index entails; if you recall, it is comprised of a number of surveys, which we aggregate in a proprietary algorithm where individual questions and surveys are weighted both in importance and whether the respondent was in management or not."

"I know, I know," replied Edward impatiently. "Come on, give me the final result and then we can go over the individual survey results."

"Okay, here we go. The result I presented to you fourteen months ago was an OHI rating of 3.2 out of 5, which is a very typical rating when I start working with most organizations. The one we did last month – are you ready? – came at 4.1, which is an improvement of twenty-two percent! I believe that is the highest jump any of our clients have had in one year!" exclaimed Doug, barely able to contain his enthusiasm.

Edward smiled broadly. "I guess you can say I am drinking the Kool- aid with a fire hose! I truly believe the turning point in this company came at the strategic planning session you facilitated twelve months ago. Those two days in Hilton Head away from the office were remarkable. Once we articulated the mission and vision statements and developed the long and short-term goals, everyone got on board this sailboat! We had such a great time sharing the results with everyone in the company, and I am convinced that today we have everyone aligned with where we are going. Like you said at the meeting, the alignment has been like iron filings to the magnet!"

In the remaining hour, Doug patiently dissected the results of all three surveys, which included: the Employee Engagement Survey, and the Team Performance Survey.

SERVANT LEADERSHIP GUIDING PRINCIPLES

Edward's experience with Pablo had been the catalyst to his self-firing and leadership transformation, which was made possible because he allowed an unlikely relationship to develop. The foundation for building a successful servant company requires building great relationships with those around you, along with other principles that help guide you in leading your team with strength, passion and love. Among these are three major principles: Love, Purpose and Discipline.

LOVE

- **Servant Leadership**: Servant leadership is about strength, not weakness. It is about making the tough decisions and at the same time being an encourager and motivator. Having this sphere of influence comes by building great relationships, by being helpful, a team builder, and by empowering others. Being committed to serving with personal humility and compassion, not blaming others, holding people accountable to goals and expectations, and having God as the foundation of your life are all pivotal to being an effective servant leader.

- **Passion**: The path towards the next level of growth and development happens when people love what they do and are passionate about the outcomes and results of their work. This shift happens when people are working with their unique gifts and talents. Therefore, identifying those gifts in an individual creates a powerful force from within.

- **Balance**: Having work/life balance is essential in keeping people engaged, motivated and to avoid burnout and reduce stress. In addition to working with God's given gift and spending relational, quality time with their spouse and kids, individuals should consciously embrace the four pillars of a self-balanced life: mind, body, soul and community.

- **Mind**: feed your mind with good literature, stay abreast of the latest technology and social issues, and exercise it with exciting puzzles and games.

- **Body**: Eat a healthy diet high in fiber and low in fat, with products grown organically, avoiding fast foods and exercising regularly.

- **Soul**: Spend each day reading the Word of God and praying. Early in the morning is a good time for that. And follow an online devotional such as www.contemplationsoftheword.com or, on Twitter, @contemplationsw.

- **Community**: Volunteer and give back to your com- munity. Select a couple of non-profit organizations and participate with your talent, time and treasure.

- **Clarity**: In the big picture of an organization, everyone needs clarity around the company's mission and vision as well as the short and long-term goals. On an individual basis, people need clarity about the job they are expected to execute with a well-written job description that includes metrics and expectations. In addition to understanding the job, it is important to match the individual's natural behavioral tendencies with the behavioral requirement of the job. In other words, do not place someone with little patience in front of a computer all day doing very detailed work.

Someone's behavioral dimensions can be found using a behavioral assessment tool such as the DISC, the Activity Vector Analysis (AVA) or the Management By Strength (MBS). The results of these assessments will guide the individual by identifying their strengths and weaknesses as well as the communication style that will be best received in managing that team member. In a team situation, knowing your team- mates' behaviors will allow for better understanding of the communication dynamics, which are often misunderstood.

- **Cohesiveness**: In one word, cohesiveness means trust. Building cohesiveness in an organization is not easy. When love exists, so does trust, and that sets the foundation for building a high-performing team. In cohesive servant teams, people really like and respect each other. They will protect each other's back and there is a level of comfort in knowing that one can be vulnerable in a team discussion without being embarrassed or criticized. On cohesive teams, team members can discuss passionately around ideological differences, reach conclusions quickly, and once a decision is made, everyone aligns and supports the final decision. Egos are left outside the room.

PURPOSE

- **Mission Statement**: The mission statement articulates the purpose for which the company exists. It answers the question of what the company does, for whom and how it is done. It should guide the actions of the organization and should serve as the North Star directing the organization's path. Mission statements should be clear, simple and straightforward. Members of an organization should not have to memorize a mission statement. It should be engrained in the company's culture. Often, mission statements are supported and strengthened by guiding principles or core values. Core values are essential tenets that articulate what a company stands for. They guide business processes, personal relationships, decision-making, and basically explain why companies do business the way they do.

- **Vision Statement**: Not to be mistaken with the Mission Statement, the Vision Statement outlines what the organization wants to be, or how it wants the world in which it operates to be as a result of what it offers. It is an aspirational long-term view and concentrates on the future. It can be a source of inspiration. For example, a non-profit organization serving the homeless might have a vision statement that reads, "A World without Homelessness." The mission will describe what it does to achieve the vision.

- **Strategy**: Once a company is absolutely clear about its purpose and has a vision of what it wants to become, leaders need to develop short and long-term goals; basically, develop the path it takes to accomplish the plan. Before getting in a room to strategize and brainstorm what these goals are, one has to analyze the current state of the company and the market conditions. Basically, the leaders of the organization have homework to do to clarify three main points: understanding the organizational profile of the company, conducting a strategic analysis of the marketplace, and comprehending the internal business intelligence.

- **Organizational Profile**: It is necessary to have a deep understanding of the company's profile. Do we have the right people and are they in the right seat in the bus? Do we have the right management systems and processes in place? Are we operating with the latest technology and integrated resources? Do we have a system and commitment to continuous improvement? Are we measuring and tracking key performance indicators? And, do we know how our customers feel about our service and products? What are they saying? Are we committed to social responsibility and taking into account how our people, our community and our environment are impacted by the business decisions we make?

- **Strategic Analysis**: Everything is changing faster than ever before. New competitors are entering the markets. With access to technology and the Internet, the barriers to entry to many industries have been obliterated. Do we know what our competitive position is in the marketplace? What are anticipated environmental forecasts that will affect how we do business and deliver our product and service? How would the current industry and customer trends affect the overall operation?

- **Business Intelligence**: It is paramount that we understand the company's internal intellectual culture. How do we make money, and what factors affect our costs and ability to be profitable? What differentiates our company in the marketplace? Are we spending resources in research and development, and do we have a culture that embraces innovation? Are we searching for blue ocean ideas? Are we being proactive in studying new markets, new geographic areas, and are we thinking beyond our borders?

- **Short and Long-Term Goals**: Once we have a thorough understanding of the company's strategy, we can then gather the leaders of the organization and chart its course.

With the company's Vision being what the company wants to become in the future, say ten years out, then working towards that goal starts by defining what the company would look like in five years and then where would it need to be in three to be on target towards the five-year goals. The three-year goals will then determine what the next twelve months goals need to be to move in that direction. Companies should then break those goals down into quarterly and monthly goals. In addition, managers should also have long and short-term business goals that align with the company's goals.

DISCIPLINE

The discipline closed-loop cycle requires four components: planning, executing, measuring and improving.

- **Planning**: An organization's process of defining its direction or specific actions requires executing a plan, determining allocation of resources, and dividing duties and processes for implementation. To determine the direction of the organization, it is necessary to understand its current position and all possible avenues through which a particular course of action should be pursued to close the gap between the current and ideal state.

- **Executing**: Greatness is achieved when the discipline of planning converges with God's given gifts and a passion for excellence to create effective execution. Executing is simply consistent and tenacious delivery of the plan that has been established. As long as the deliverables of the plan are realistic and attainable, successful execution can be achieved. Here is where you make it happen.

- **Measuring**: Well-executed plans have to be measured. Metrics are a crucial but sometimes overlooked component of strategy and implementation. Implementing a plan with no measurement of success is like running your heart out in a track and field race with no finish line to mark the end point and having no official stop clock to measure or compare finish times. Tools of measurement can differ depending on the type of strategy, including percent of market share, sales increase, return on investment (ROI) and profit margins, to name a few.

- **Improving**: Improving overall organizational performance should be an ongoing goal of any great servant leadership organization. This can be achieved through the adoption of technology, introduction of business systems, and utilization of more effective processes and procedures. These are ways in which a company can ensure continuous growth and improvement in employees and the company.

THE TECHNICAL STUFF

S o the question then becomes how does a company improve overall performance 22% in one year? We are not talking here about having a great financial year that yields higher profits.

We are talking about a holistic and sustainable improvement of human capital alignment, operational efficiencies and measurable objectives. This is not change management; this is about putting in place systems and processes that are consistent in nature and where members of the organization speak the same business vocabulary. And yes, it starts with the CEO and the leadership team.

It starts by understanding what matters most in the organization, which is the people that work there and make it happen day after day.

It has been said over and over again that the biggest asset in an organization is its people. True. We can expand by adding that it is motivated, engaged and passionate people who feel appreciated, feel like they are growing personally and are operating with a consistent management structure where servant leadership values are embraced. And where there is a culture of continuous improvement, there is alignment with the organization's mission and vision.

To quantify improvement, one must have a benchmark to compare against. As a culture, we measure everything, or so it seems. Therefore, it makes sense that if our goal is to have an organization with people who are growing and improving, then we need a starting point, a baseline.

Using the principles of Love, Purpose and Discipline described in this book as the foundation for organizational growth and improvement, one must start by addressing where we are as individuals and as teams before addressing where the company stands.

Here is a servant leadership survey and a servant team survey that can be downloaded from the website shown at the end of the book.

SERVANT LEADERSHIP SURVEY

1	Strongly Disagree
2	Disagree
3	Unsure
4	Agree
5	Strongly Agree

1. Is passionate about positive impact on people

1 2 3 4 5

2. Builds trustful and loving relationships with people

1 2 3 4 5

3. Is a great listener and provides thoughtful feedback

1 2 3 4 5

4. Resolves conflicts in a caring way

1 2 3 4 5

5. Is a visionary with established direction and purpose

1 2 3 4 5

6. Empowers people and holds them accountable

1 2 3 4 5

7. Motivates people to achieve highest results

1 2 3 4 5

8. Rewards and praises good performance

1 2 3 4 5

9. Shines light on others

1 2 3 4 5

10. Does not blame

1 2 3 4 5

11. Builds respectful cohesive teams

1 2 3 4 5

12. Is patient

1 2 3 4 5

13. Serves with humility

1 2 3 4 5

14. Is helpful

1 2 3 4 5

15. Is empathetic and caring

1 2 3 4 5

16. Recognizes others strengths and weaknesses

1 2 3 4 5

17. Is disciplined about planning and executing

1 2 3 4 5

18. Is disciplined about measuring results

1 2 3 4 5

19. Is disciplined about continuous improvement

1 2 3 4 5

20. God is the foundation of their life

1 2 3 4 5

SERVANT TEAM SURVEY

1. Team members love and care for each other

   ☐1 ☐2 ☐3 ☐4 ☐5

2. Members are passionate about their work

   ☐1 ☐2 ☐3 ☐4 ☐5

3. The team is cohesive with clear direction

   ☐1 ☐2 ☐3 ☐4 ☐5

4. Team members are always respectful

   ☐1 ☐2 ☐3 ☐4 ☐5

5. Members roles are clearly understood

   ☐1 ☐2 ☐3 ☐4 ☐5

6. There is peer accountability

   ☐1 ☐2 ☐3 ☐4 ☐5

7. Members debate ideological differences without egos

   ☐1 ☐2 ☐3 ☐4 ☐5

8. Team is goal-directed and persistent

   ☐1 ☐2 ☐3 ☐4 ☐5

9. Members are committed to the success of the team

   ☐1 ☐2 ☐3 ☐4 ☐5

10. There is total absence of cynicism and sarcasm

    ☐1 ☐2 ☐3 ☐4 ☐5

How do you rate? How does your team rate? Make a list of yours and your team's scores less than 4. You now have a baseline to work from!

Use this information to start your company's servant leadership improvement process by creating action plans around every one of the items that did not rate above a 3. Work with your team to analyze the team score and in a collaborative process, discuss what is and is not working, what needs improvement and how to strengthen the leadership of the items that scored above a 3. This will give the team an opportunity to team build, get to know each other better and start on the road of trust, clarity and cohesiveness.

This work is not easy, so consider a third party facilitator to achieve better results.

Remember Edward and the overall improvement of the Organizational Health Index his mentor, Doug, presented? Achieving comprehensive organizational improvement requires three main components:

1. A company comprehensive evaluation to identify gaps and challenges followed by a

prioritized list of recommended improvements and changes.

2. Strategic implementation of the recommendations.

3. Company-wide employee training in consistent management processes and systems.

Surveys can be found at
www.fireyourselfmovement.com/surveys

About the Author

Willy Stewart, A native of Colombia, received his bachelor's and master's degrees in Civil Engineering from NC State University. In1994 he founded Stewart Engineering known today as Stewart with multiple offices throughout North Carolina and Virginia offering a wide variety of services, including land planning and design, structural engineering, transportation, geomatics and construction services.

Mr. Stewart through his management consulting firm, i2 Integrated Intelligence, advises CEO's and leaders of diverse industries how to optimize the integration of culture and business intelligence.

He began the Fire Yourself Movement, which is aimed at a new generation of business leaders rising up to demonstrate their strength through service and love.

stewartinc.com
i2integratedintelligence.com
fireyourselfmovement.com

CPSIA information can be obtained
at www.ICGtesting.com
Printed in the USA
FFOW04n1140310318
46085589-47047FF